Adults and Their Parents in Family Therapy
A NEW DIRECTION IN TREATMENT

Adults and Their Parents in Family Therapy
A NEW DIRECTION IN TREATMENT

Lee Headley, Ph.D.

With a Foreword by Virginia M. Satir

PLENUM PRESS • NEW YORK AND LONDON

Library of Congress Cataloging in Publication Data

Headley, Lee.
　Adults and their parents in family therapy.

　Includes index.
　1. Family psychotherapy. I. Title. [DNLM: 1. Family therapy. WM430 H433r]
RC488.5.H4　　　　　　　　　616.8'915　　　　　　　　　77-13990
ISBN 0-306-31087-5

© 1977 Lee Headley

Plenum Press, New York
A Division of Plenum Publishing Corporation
227 West 17th Street, New York, N.Y. 10011

All rights reserved

No part of this book may be reproduced, stored in a retrieval system or transmitted, in any form or by any means, electronic, mechanical, photocopying, microfilming, recording, or otherwise, without written permission

Printed in the United States of America

To my daughter

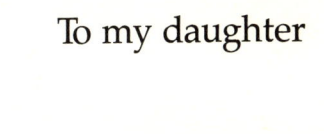

Foreword

In 1951 I saw my first family for therapeutic reasons. It resulted from a whole series of apparent accidents and coincidences. Seeing families in 1951 was clearly a departure from accepted therapeutic behavior, and in many quarters of the world I was looked upon as a freak.

Now in 1977 the world looks like quite a different place, therapeutically speaking. Many of us in the early 1950s were working in the "closet," and we did not know of the existence of each other. It was only later that we came together to share our new and controversial findings and risk open discussion of them. A lot has happened since then.

In her book, Dr. Headley gives a brief but quite comprehensive overview of the changes in thinking about treating a troubled person. I would say that all of you who have had anything to do with helping a troubled person have been aware of the relationship between correct perceptions and feelings in the individual and the early experiences in childhood. That fact is not new. Since the advent of family therapy, where intergenerational boundaries were bridged with people being in the presence of one another, an important fact has begun to emerge. Perceptions of children about their parents, and vice versa, when confronted and understood, were often found to be based on serious misunderstandings. I can still remember people looking at me with a sense of awe and a reported feeling of anxiety as I described confrontations between the generations in the family interviews.

I view Dr. Headley's book as a resource volume about using the sources. Dr. Headley is obviously a sensitive yet tough, reality-minded therapist, who is willing to engage people in the basic things that trouble them, and to engage persistently in helping them to come to a new reality.

Perhaps without meaning it, many of us as therapists have been so afraid to deal with this in other people because we still feel very much like little children in relation to our own parents. As Dr. Headley points out, we could get to the part of being able to express our anger and resentment, but we had no way to go beyond that. While that left us free in relation to the burden we carried, it did not necessarily make for any better relationships with our own parents.

Dr. Murray Bowen has for some time now been urging his patients to find and connect anew with the members of their nuclear family. Through a method I call family reconstruction, which I implement through the medium of role play, I have tried to help people come to what I call their personhood with their own parents. A natural consequence of the family reconstruction is for people to make really new contacts with their family members if they are still living. If they are dead, it is an opportunity for them to give a new basis to old situations and thus feel on a different level with them.

One of the most important things that Dr. Headley's book can accomplish is that it can give courage to the therapist to attempt to build the bridges between the generations in a face-to-face way, and at the same time to give hope to all of us that much of what we perceive about our parents and about ourselves is essentially built on a house of cards—valid for the ways we perceive things, but not valid for the total human situation.

Virginia M. Satir

Preface

I began doing a great deal of family therapy when I was working with Dr. Don D. Jackson, who at the time was director of the psychiatry department at the Palo Alto Medical Clinic and starting the Mental Research Institute in Palo Alto, California. I had been a consultant in group therapy at the psychiatry department and had worked with Don on cases, as he was no longer practicing psychoanalysis in the classical mode. Mental Research Institute had such interesting personalities as Gregory Bateson, John Weakland, Jay Haley, and Virginia Satir.

Virginia Satir originated the Family Therapy Training Unit at Mental Research Institute. Under her leadership, the unit became a vibrant and exciting mecca to members of the various human services professions and it achieved an outstanding national reputation. From some years now Virginia has been teaching and demonstrating communications skills in Europe, emphasizing that families are the microcosms of the world system. This book carries a somewhat similar message that those who leave the family home bring with them ideas of marriage, parenthood, and personal relationships that affect their marital partners, their children, employers, and whomever they may encounter. Those ideas need not be fixed, however, and may be altered beneficially for parents, their adult children, and their families.

My private practice began after I started working with Don and Virginia and included individual therapy, marital counseling, group therapy, and considerable family therapy work. I was also a consultant at the Santa Clara County Mental Health Clinics, Children's Health Council, Family Service, and various other clinics and agencies. Many of the people in distress whom I saw both in my own office and at these agencies seemed so enmeshed in dysfunctional families that I kept emphasizing the futility of dealing only with an individual, while other family influences were obviously not being touched. This impressed me forcibly in marriage situations, and so from those early times I began seeing older parents and brothers and sisters, as well as any other relatives who appeared to be important in the situation. This method seemed to work faster and produce a more harmonious family circle.

The experiences over these years have led to the ideas expressed in this book. I continue to use the method in my present setting, which is a rather large private psychiatric clinic offering services to children and adults—the Family and Child Psychiatric Medical Clinic, San Jose, California.

The following pages will detail, and illustrate through cases, my belief that although families may have had frictions that resulted in adult children with handicapping personal traits, on poor terms with their parents, there is a strong need and will for adult children and their aging parents to heal their relationships. Others have attempted to help patients improve and readjust their interactions with their parents. Murray Bowen[1] encourages and coaches his patients to visit their parents with the aim of changing the relationship when it is hurtful. Virginia Satir's method is family reconstruction role play, in which others take the

---

[1] Bowen, Murray. Towards the differentiation of a self in one's own family. In James Framo (Ed.), *Family interaction*. New York: Springer, 1972.

roles of family members. James Framo has a recent article describing a treatment approach with the original family. At Mental Research Institute, Louise Sorensen headed a project on aging, which included adult children to consider and help in the problems of the parents' aging. In this instance, the main focus was on aiding the parents.

The aim of psychotherapy has been to overcome handicapping past learning experiences in childhood. Concepts of marital behavior are absorbed in childhood families and are often transmitted into duplicate behavior in the adult child's marriage. We are well aware that perceptions of self and perceptions of others result from early family interactions and that these perceptions may persist to affect the individual's life in an adverse way no matter how much the circumstances and the self have changed.

My thesis is that relearning toward a more positive functioning can take place with the conjoint participation of the adult child, the parents, and other family members for mutual welfare. The relearning takes place directly at the source of the original relationships, the family, rather than through the often lengthy relearning in traditional psychotherapy. Not that this method is easy. On the contrary, it requires considerable skill and care. It requires experience in regular family therapy concerning dependent children before attempting it. However, I feel it should be an alternate treatment choice for all experienced therapists. This book attempts to distill my experience and techniques for those who may wish to use this method of treatment.

Lee Headley

Acknowledgments

I wish to thank my good friends Jean Louis Brindamour of Strawberry Hill Press, San Francisco, and Norma Crockett, formerly of Stanford University Counselling Center, for their invaluable help and encouragement to me in writing this book. I extend thanks also to Virginia Satir and John Weakland, who have been friends and colleagues throughout the years.

L. H.

Contents

1 • Freud to Family Therapy   17
2 • Goals of the Family, Goals of Psychotherapy   31
3 • Patient, Parent, and Therapist Attitudes toward Conjoint Meetings   43
4 • Inclusion of Parents in Marital Therapy   63
5 • Inclusion of Parents in Adult Individual Therapy   79
6 • Siblings Join in Therapy of the Adult Child   95
7 • Typical Transactions with Parents   103
8 • Hazardous Situations   125
9 • Discussion of Sexual Problems with Older Parents   135
10 • Two Additional Uses of the Method   147
11 • Procedures and Follow-Up with Patient and Parent   163
12 • Conclusion   179
     Index   191

procedures have been greatly refined and have been able to provide early relief and improvement for many psychological difficulties.

This book proposes to discuss in some detail a method for the treatment of marital and adult psychological and behavioral problems utilizing members of the original childhood family—parents, siblings, and other relatives. The people in such treatment are not dependent upon, or living with, the family. Before discussing that method, however, it would be well to consider the historical perspective of methods of psychological treatment in order to see some of its contributing origins.

Psychoanalysis, the original Western form of psychotherapy, occupies a prominent and respected place in the field. Freud's theories concerning the Oedipus complex, libidinal energy, ego, etc., are fairly well known to the general public. Less well known is the process of free association of ideas, which is calculated to elicit feelings and attitudes that are guarded, repressed, or unconscious, and that impel the patient to behavior or modes of thinking and feeling that do not work out well for him. The process of free association and the analyst's removal of himself from interaction with the patient encourage the patient to project those feelings that he had toward significant others in his life onto the analyst. The so-called transference is a vital tool in psychoanalysis. The therapist offers a clarification of the patient's projections and, through the patient's transference of feelings, demonstrates to the patient that his assumptions about others may not be true. Further, through transference, he may have a corrective experience of a benign and constructive relationship with an authority (parental-like) figure.

Underlying psychoanalytic theory is Freud's idea that there are instinctual and emotional drives that go through phases in the process of an individual's growth. The individual may become stuck at any one of these phases and thus be distorted and underdeveloped in his emotional

1

Freud to Family Therapy

A great many Americans today are seeking psychotherapeutic help for their personal problems in living. Most of these people are adults, working and self-supporting, frequently with a family of several children. They are distinguished from their fellow citizens by the fact that they have decided to seek some professional assistance rather than struggle through their problems themselves. They may be having marital discord, depressed feelings, unsuccessful human relationships, a sense of isolation and frustration, difficulty with fellow workers, in-law problems, or general dissatisfaction with their goals and achievements in life. Some of these complaints are chronic, and some are in crisis conditions. Most of the above problems are experienced by others in the community, but for their own reasons they continue attempting to cope with their problems on their own. They too might be interested in some psychological services were it not for the fact that psychotherapy derived from psychiatry; psychiatry in turn, had its initial focus on seriously mentally ill persons, often hospitalized. Although psychiatry has developed to serve many other populations, there is still an aura of sickness and failure that clings to psychotherapists and the people they serve. This is regrettable because psychotherapeutic growth. Usually this is a result of some inhibitory actions on the part of his parents or the family group. Since this is an intrapsychic phenomenon, the analyst is concerned with the patient's perceptions of his experiences and what he feels is the basis of his style of functioning in life. Classical psychoanalysis is essentially a monadic approach, for relatives, parents, or significant others are not included in the process of psychotherapy. Freud himself preferred not to deal with parents or family members. The patient's reporting of his experiences is, therefore, an exclusive (possibly distorted) view since much of what went on in his early life is forgotten and much else is cryptic to him, for he can only infer what may have been the motivations for various behaviors. All those other factors in the family circle that might have some bearing on the etiology of his difficulty are therefore unavailable to the patient and to the therapist.

Psychoanalysis has been a pioneer in the path of developing psychotherapeutic skills. Originating in work with seriously ill persons, it has tended to deal more with adults who are functioning well enough to be able to pursue professions and maintain themselves independently of their childhood families. Psychoanalysis has been of great benefit to many individuals in the resolution of their difficulties. Perhaps the chief criticism of the method has been directed toward the length of time required for treatment, its expense, and the paucity of psycholanalytic time available to those who would like to have it. The number of trained psychoanalysts in the United States is quite small. Few members are added to the profession each year as they complete training through the various psychoanalytic institutes. If one assumes the average length of treatment time for the individual to be two to three years, it is easy to calculate that with only a few thousand psychoanalysts in the country, very little psychoanalytic treatment time is, in fact, available.

Subsequent therapists and theorists such as Alfred Adler

and Harry S. Sullivan added more concern with the social context of the patient and with interactions within the social circle of the patient. The life situations, past and present, of the individual not only are seen as pertinent as to causation of his personal difficulties but are also perceived to be significant factors that can inhibit, circumscribe, slant, or enhance the ways in which he may express his emotions, develop his ego, and express his will and drive. Relationships now can be viewed as reciprocally reactive forces that can be used outside of the professional dyad. Along with relationship therapy and more attention to interactions between people, the therapist became a more active participant in the process of therapy and was no longer remote, but instead appeared as an individual personality reacting to and with the patient and interested in knowing about the activities of people who could contribute to the patient's improvement. The interactional view of psychotherapy came about in approximately the same period of time as the development of relativity theories in physics and systems theories in the biological and sociological sciences.

Relationship therapy theories and an interactional focus contributed to the growth and development of group psychotherapy and the therapeutic community in hospital settings. In these situations, the person widens his contacts beyond a therapist to other persons who join him in a like endeavor. The same transactions are occurring, however. The person is expressing and clarifying his views about himself and his typical ways of behavior, aided by feedback from his fellow members. He is again trying new ways of reacting and behaving, from which will come a sense of growth and maturation, a new and more positive definition of self. Group members may seem more benign and flexible persons to relate to than were childhood family members.

A comparatively recent development is the growth of encounter groups where strangers meet to experience emotional transactions with one another. The emphasis in such groups is on interaction and experiences of feeling; cognitive experiences are downgraded and usually any intellectual appraisals are rejected. The group members hope that some emotional catharsis will take place and that some new attitudes about themselves as "feeling" human beings will occur, and that useful inputs of others in their environment will be emotionally incorporated and synthesized into their personality. Those who are psychologically isolated from others or constricted in the expression of their feelings, positive and negative, are the frequent members of such groups. Generally, such persons are from childhood families where expression of emotion and reaction to others was prohibited, sterile, or severely restricted. These persons are consequently trying to overcome the effects of parent–child or sibling–child interactions, within the present-day context, by being with (they hope) more reachable individuals. The encounter group members become surrogates for the individual's childhood family figures, which may result in more fortunate outcomes. Many persons are substantially aided by such encounter groups when led and supervised by trained professionals. At the other end of the scale are acute breakdowns by those who dangerously abandon their defenses in encounter groups or marathons where proper safeguards by professional persons are absent. These individuals find themselves rejected or sharply criticized by the group and are vulnerable to shock and disintegration of their customary defensive system.

Another hazard observed in this approach to therapeutic change is the development of the encounter addict. Such a person continues to attend encounter meetings, enjoying the temporary intimacy and resulting "highs" from the warmth and freedom of the exchanges but often without being able to integrate these new experiences into his everyday contacts, including his present family. It may be that the techniques and approaches used in the group seem silly or inconsequential to the significant others in his life, so that he returns to the group's structured environment for a new infusion of emotional experience and reassurance.

One of the most significant developments in psychiatric treatment is the psychotherapeutic modality known as conjoint family therapy. Nathan Ackerman was an early leader in this field, and Gregory Bateson, Don Jackson, Jay Haley, and John Weakland have contributed much to the establishment of theory underlying conjoint family therapy and the functioning of families. Techniques growing out of this theoretical approach have now included many interventions that the practitioner can employ, in meeting conjointly with the total family in his office, for the resolution of family conflicts and misunderstandings. Family therapy changes the emphasis and focus of therapy from the description of individuals and families as sick to that of a dysfunctional family, which implies that changes and improvements are possible and are a part of the ongoing processes of family life.

Much of the original work, as well as that of the present, centered around the schizophrenic patient, who is traditionally difficult to treat and who represents a large portion of those patients who are statistically listed as chronic hospital cases, occupying one-half of the country's chronic hospital beds. Here traditional psychoanalysis had been only minimally successful; other therapeutic techniques had not fared much better. The work of Bateson, Jackson, Haley, and Weakland produced the "double bind" theory. This theory is family-based and postulates that a dysfunctional family issues contradictory messages to the "identified patient," the person who exhibits personal or social problems. One of these messages is spoken and overt. The other is often covert and conveyed by tone, facial expression, or body movement. The patient is enjoined from commenting on the discrepancy of the messages either by denial of his observations by the parents and other family members or by ridicule and condemnation of the patient's ability to perceive correctly. The identified patient is usually a child still dependent on the family, or a psychologically disabled member of the family who is hospitalized or in some dependent position that means he cannot leave the system to break the bind.

Inherent in conjoint family therapy is the recognition of the family as a system with well-understood rules and typical styles of communication. Conjoint family therapy has developed greatly since its beginnings in theory, detailing of therapeutic instructions, and examinations of family processes. Family therapy investigators have done much research and treatment of specific problems, such as asthmatic children, delinquents, or drug abusers.

From these researches and investigations have come two other important areas—communication theories and theories of how family processes affect and determine how children grow and mature psychologically within the family. Virginia Satir's book, *Peoplemaking*,[1] describes in detail with much color and drama how the powerful interactions between all family members shape a child's perception of himself, of others, and of the world around him. The book concerns itself with how one can understand and guide the child toward full and satisfactory participation with others while retaining his own unique individuality. The emphasis is in the direction of creating healthy families and individuals. This is a fortunate direction that psychotherapy has taken—an emphasis upon growth and maximization rather than on the crippled and deplorable condition of the individual. "Well family" clinics may yet become part of the health sciences.

It is to be noted that in conjoint family therapy, remedial and constructive changes are attempted with the original authors of the family. This means *all* members of the family. They are seen conjointly so that everyone can perceive

[1]Satir, Virginia. *Peoplemaking*. Palo Alto: Science and Behavior Books, 1972.

and experience transactions as they happen. Whenever the child or individual has absorbed attitudes from his family that are disabling to him intrapsychically or in his social relationships, attention is directed to the original and ongoing transactions that adversely affect him. The therapeutic intervention of the professional is directed toward unambiguously clarifying what the interpersonal exchange consists of and what the motivations are behind it. When the exchange is, or was, harmful, the family can initiate a new course of action by mutual consent. If the interactions were based on lack of information or incorrect information, these can be jointly explored and corrected. Sometimes family members know that things are not going well but they do not know what to do to improve the situation. Other times, parents or other family members are engaging in maneuvers to maintain their own feelings of self-worth, dominance, security, etc., by rigid control.

Families have by their very nature an active interest and vital stake in the welfare of all of its members. This factor can be profitably used to redirect the family processes if they have gone awry.

The elements of psychoanalytic theory that are most important to our discussion are the superego and fixations at levels of ego development. The superego relates primarily to the actions of parents that inform the child of his goals and limitations and what he should think of himself and others. Beyond the parents is the culture that over a long period of time has determined what and how parents *should* teach their children. The child, having grown up and incorporated parental ideas of role and expectations in life, may or may not manage his life constructively depending on what use he can make of what he has.

The family therapy concept of homeostasis, family systems, and family rules enlarges the view of who and what constitutes the superego limiting the ego. Systems theory provides a means of understanding why certain role behavior becomes assigned to certain individuals, plus a recognition that systems and roles in the web of relationships are alterable.

The thesis of this book is that beneficial changes are possible for personal or marital difficulties of independent adults through involvement of older parents (superego figures). A new family balance and different family rules evolve through restructuring the relationships of persons who are now peers—the adult child and the older parent.

Development of Marital Therapy

Marital therapy for troubled couples in conflict has become accepted and respected. That there is a burgeoning interest in theory and techniques of treatment, and evaluation of effectiveness for marital therapy, is evidenced by the increase in professional articles. Alan Gurman[2] reviewed such publications for a period of the last forty years and found that the number of articles concerning professional treatment of marital couples began to exhibit an abrupt increase in 1961, doubled in number in 1967 to 1972, and tripled in the total period 1964 to 1972. Three-quarters of the extant publications have appeared in the last ten years. These figures do not include, of course, the popular articles found in women's magazines, which devote large sections of their press to marital problems. The content of these professional articles is increasingly in the direction of new techniques and evaluation of the effectiveness of marital therapy. The trend appears to be empirical rather than theoretical, and is concerned with those approaches that reduce the length of treatment and give substantial results.

Many couples initially sought help for their marital problems from their religious counselors. Until comparatively recently, however, such persons were not psychologically trained and then, and now, may have convictions about

[2]Gurman, Alan S. Marital therapy: Emerging trends in research and practise. *Family Process*, 1973, *12* (1, March).

their obligations to preserve marriages at all costs or to shape them in certain directions. These orientations were also observed in some of the early training institutions for marital counseling where practitioners were to "treat the marriage" rather than its members. Such approaches might be termed more authoritative than participatory.

Treatment of marital problems has been affected by, and also affects, the ongoing theoretical and practical developments in individual psychotherapy. The practice of treating marital partners separately or via the use of two separate therapists was allied to the earlier methods of psychoanalytic treatment and followed the monadic model. It was the natural bias for those therapists who were trained in individual therapy and who felt such patient–therapist relationships to be manageable. Since it relied upon individual therapy for each member of the marriage, their joint functioning did not always improve.

Development of theories that saw personal difficulties as interpersonal, interactional, and socially-based led to the growth of group therapy for marital couples. Couples groups provide a wider view of how others interpret and act out the marital model, and permit inputs from other group members about the values, emotional stance, and behavior of the couple. Now the man or woman who could not convey to the spouse how certain behavior implied a certain attitude could hear other group participants make the same kind of deduction. When partners are in conflict and concerned with one-upmanship, they often cannot "hear" the other person or credit him with a valid idea. In some ways, group comments offer more support and are more effective than if the therapist made a similar observation to the couple, especially in cases where one spouse was determined to cling to his view at all costs. The therapeutic transactions in these groups are between the therapist as a benign authority and group members: The group members may represent parental figures, siblings, or other significant figures in life experiences. Couple group therapy contributes a greater awareness of how other people can function, enlarges the field for potential adjustments, desensitizes the couple to feelings of failure and therefore need for concealment, and offers a medium for experience in making new transactions with others.

However, what one often finds is the spouse who has a fairly deep-seated problem arising from childhood experiences. These are often difficult to deal with in group therapy because of limited time, needs of others, and the inappropriateness of concentrating too much on one person's difficulty.

Behavior modifications techniques as applied to marital problems are primarily educational and experiential. The therapist is not so involved in personal transactions with a participant or the couple, but rather by necessity assumes an authoritative role. Behavioral modification may seem much more tangible and definite to the couple having trouble, when they are uncertain of the roots of their conflicts. Many people feel safer when trying concrete suggestions than they do when asked to explore their own attitudes and consider what the genesis of such attitudes is. Operant conditioning certainly offers much benefit in learning new ways to cope but probably its greater benefit has been to children of the couple.

Family systems theory greatly stimulated the procedure of seeing marital couples conjointly. Such interviews are usually laden with rapid exchanges, accusations and counteraccusations, and attempts to justify and buttress the individual's position. Systems theory makes it possible to see the rules of the system and the complementary behavior that keeps it in balance when otherwise it might appear quite baffling. It is soon possible, moreover, to perceive the shadows of previous marital systems deriving from the couple's own parents and now influencing, consciously or unconsciously, their way of relating to one another. Children learn about social roles and social behavior from observing the models of husband and wife, mother, father, discipliner, host and hostess, etc., provided by their parents. What the parents *said* should be done made much less impact, partially because parents' behavior was often different from what their own rules dictated. Couples often find, to their complete dismay, that they are duplicating their parents' marital system, something that they had decided years ago as children that they would never do. The process, generally, is that the child observes something going on with his parent or parents that he thinks is bad or unfair or destructive. Through his teen years he reminds himself that he is not going to live like that and very consciously tries to choose a mate who seems to offer a different mode of behavior and a different set of values. Commonly, not too long after the marriage, a spouse or couple starts duplicating the same attitudes and behavior that he or she saw at home.

Then comes the question of what to do. The patient himself seems stuck with the problem and ruefully criticizes himself. The therapist may encourage him to consciously fight against any behavior that is destructive to the other spouse or to the relationship. There is usually extensive self-examination, which leads to a fair intellectual understanding of the problem but often not to any viable emotional alteration. Usually the patient does try hard and conscientiously to alter his attitudes and behavior but makes little headway. If the other member of the marriage alters his or her behavior, however, the results are usually initial conflict, then inability to adjust to the other spouse's behavior. The process is apt to be slow and upsetting and sometimes leads to crises like separation.

Often, however, spouses do not really perceive that their behavior is learned from parental models either because they have persuaded themselves that they have made the proper corrections or because, sometimes, the parents are seen as problem-free. The other spouse often sees a totally different picture of the parents, and this leads to arguments over who is right, accusations of bias, and surges of protective emotion about the rightness and goodness of the spouse's parents. When this happens the therapist may gain information from other family members. But this has the disadvantage that it might start conflicts with other relatives who may be called disloyal, biased, or taking sides with one spouse. Probably the therapist will not be able to determine the facts without seeing the parents himself.

It then appears that one is dealing with a marriage system that derives from an older and prior marriage system and that presumably there were other marriage systems from even earlier generations that left their imprint. I believe that these inherited-by-learning systems may be therapeutically interrupted to the benefit of the present couple and their parents by including the older parents in the treatment process.

2

Goals of the Family, Goals of Psychotherapy

Goals of the Family

Consider the functions of the family. The primary members, mother and father, have been brought together by complementary needs. They need the sense of fulfillment, of security, of sharing, of belonging that the different characteristics of men and women bring to marriages. Entrance of a child may threaten these needs on the part of both parents, and one of the first "normal" crises of a marriage and an established family concerns the integration of that child into the already existing family system. Parents are keenly aware of the responsibility to assist a child to grow and develop in a healthy manner, physically, emotionally, and socially. They attempt to build self-esteem, responsibility, and competence in the child toward eventual independent maturity. Meanwhile, they must maintain their own self-esteem and individuality and obtain satisfaction of their own needs. Sharing involves the need for all to cooperate in dealing with the natural stresses that occur in life, and to be helpful to one another in seeking alternate solutions to the problems that arise. As those crises occur, the family needs to develop appropriate defenses against the anxiety engendered by uncertain or threatening reality situations and relationships. In this process, members need to support each other in various ways to maintain health, communication, and participation. Further, the individuals within the family need to retain their individuality and to encourage the others to develop in their individual ways without destroying, damaging, or absorbing, other individuals in the corporate family group. Implied in this is the eventual freedom of the child to graduate from the family and establish himself in his own life-style, ideally with the understanding of the family that this is his right as long as it is not injurious to anyone else, even though that style may be strange or unpalatable to the parents.

While this is the primary organic and social function of the family, its mode will be determined by the idiosyncratic ideas and abilities of the individual members. Further, they will be affected by the social situation that surrounds them. These may be ethnic and cultural factors that from long historical roots still dominate thinking and standards in families. Further, social events that surround the family inevitably make their mark and exert an influence on what becomes important or unimportant in attitude and behavior. Millions of families were fundamentally affected by the Great Depression of the 1930s, and many family members continue to respond to the traumas of those times via attitudes toward their peers, their children, and their relatives. World War II set in train another set of values that echoes through three generations. The affluent times of the sixties have demonstrably affected family processes. The most notable is probably the scorn for money and material possessions that many young people today act out, most prevalently in the hippie culture.

Families also reverberate to the prevailing philosophies of their day and their social context. The familiar "children should be seen and not heard" is a reflection of one philosophy pertaining to children's rights. Conversely, parents today are attempting to cope with children who take an opposite view and believe that children have equal rights with parents. This philosophy is currently visible in some high schools where children determine their course of study, and in some avant-garde colleges where students have a voice in deciding not only what the curriculum should be but also who should be admitted to the college.

Greater economic resources and social opportunities now available to women, plus increased questioning of the basis of marriage, have resulted in new versions of marriage and new definitions of respective roles for young people. Marriages may not have a legal ceremony, or the contract between the persons is solemnized in their own particular terms. Responsibilities and work within the family are more apt to be equally shared by the couple.

These philosophical variations and the resultant discrepancies in the way that parents experienced their own child training versus what needs to be done today in coping with children can be as disturbing and baffling to parents as were the harsh realities of life for wandering dust bowl refugees in the Great Depression. Many parents attempt to meet these changing reality circumstances and attitudinal shifts by standing pat on what had been taught them, rather than trying to sort out the durable new from the welter of fads and philosophies.

Many ideas that are current in our culture are derivations of Judeo-Christian ideas, such as freedom of individual choice, equality of persons, and independence of thought and action. Still, they may have many shades of meaning and be differently interpreted in different parts of the country. Behavioral ideals in Boston are apt to be different from the norms of Los Angeles.

All this makes great demands upon the resources of parents. The outcomes may well depend upon the ability of a couple to work well together and to be flexible in meeting new contingencies.

Goals of Psychotherapy

What are the goals of psychotherapy? They appear to be much like the goals of the family. Nathan Ackerman states that "psychotherapy itself has achieved a wide range of definitions, depending on the differing situational contexts of the relationship between patient and therapist. In a general way, it may be described as a systematic procedure by which one person, professionally trained, seeks to influence through psychological means the emotional functions of another person, the patient, for his health. The task has two facets: the elimination of suffering and disabled functioning, and the enhancement of the patient's ability to fulfill himself as a person and as a member of society."[1]

One definition of a successful outcome of this process is that the patient has gained "insight." Considerable experience has now accumulated to cause doubt that such attainment of insight will ensure benefits such as more successful interaction with others and freedom to change life-styles and redirect energies to self-fulfillment. It is not uncommon for patients to perceive that they have developed, for example, a self-punishing personality and that its roots lie in the experiences with childhood family. They see that they continuously involve themselves in more such relationships, which punish and hurt them. Such patients often do not move on to change their modus operandi but employ their insight as an excuse for not doing anything further. "That's the way I am" or "Well, that's the way I was trained" are the kind of remarks with which they turn off any further progress. Insight must therefore be combined with changes in the way they manage their lives.

Ackerman further says, "There is increasing understanding of the criteria by which a true psychotherapeutic change is induced. Such change is expressed as a series of shifts in feeling, in perception, in meaning, in bodily expe-

[1] Ackerman, Nathan W. *Treating the troubled family.* New York: Basic Books, 1966. p. 52.

Goals of the Family, Goals of Psychotherapy

rience, and in the integration of personality into the appropriate role positions in the group. In other words, in the last analysis, cure is measured by the development of a new and more effective set of relationships and corresponding social action."

Consider the goals of the family for its child as previously outlined. Parents are seeking ideally to foster and teach their offspring self-esteem, responsibility, independence, cooperation, dealing effectively with stress, sharing, communication, and individuality. The therapist's goals are essentially the same, although he comes late on the scene and many parts of the family's goals may have already been reached. Most likely, however, the person who comes for help has not learned self-esteem or has learned that he "should" have low self-esteem. Probably he is not too effective in communicating his feelings, or his perception of others' feelings, or his needs and his aspirations. He may not deal very well with stress. In fact, he has sought help because he cannot cope with his particular stress. He often has problems about his identity—who is he? Is he a good person? Or perhaps he is certain that he is a bad person.

In the preceding discussion of various modes of therapy for individuals and marital couples, the common denominator of relationship therapy seems to be that the therapist is providing, through his transactions with patient or patients, *a surrogate parental role*. He stimulates self-awareness and encourages the self-esteem of the patient. This may involve the correction of much information supplied to the patient by his family members. Therapists emphasize the responsibility for the patient's own actions, including his willingness to change for the better. Independence is the ultimate goal of the therapist who wishes the patient to be functioning well in his sphere, able to go out on his own. Cooperation is inherent in the therapeutic working relationship and should be extended to the members of the patient's present family or friends. The focus of much therapeutic effort is directed toward dealing effectively with stress via support, encouragement, pointing out alternatives, and requiring the patient to draw upon his own abilities. Clear communication is the stuff of the patient–therapist exchange. It furthers the processes of sharing and of enhancing the person's sense of unique and valuable individuality. These functions and transactions of the therapist usually are effective and result in considerable improvement in the patient's sense of well-being. He gets more out of life and does well in his relationships with significant others, as well as with the larger world around him.

However, there are some disadvantages to the procedures in psychotherapeutic work by which patients are helped to reevaluate that part of their childhood upbringing that may have been crippling and inhibiting. Generally, the patient perceives the errors in judgment and faulty actions of his parents and then goes through a period of anger and resentment at them. He reshapes his perceptions of himself and his attitudes toward the world to the benefit of his present day-to-day life. In doing so, he achieves the separation of a more complete sort from his original parental figures. This may leave him with a residue of ill feeling or resentment, which rises periodically to plague him. He may also feel cheated and one-down in comparison to others in his family, such as siblings, and one-down as he compares himself to others in the world. This gives rise to some discomfort psychically. Further, while healthy psychological separation from his parents in the process of psychotherapy is essential to his growth, individuation, and maturation, there is a nagging feeling of loss since one's original sense of belonging arose from connection with family and parents.

Parents of such adult patients are seldom heard from and therapists have no way of knowing what they feel about the change in their adult child. One assumes that these parents may often feel baffled, hurt, or anxious when their relationship to their adult child changes. This would be particularly true either if their adult child severed the relationship or if their bonds to him began to seem uncomfortably thin and strained.

Therapists do not have a social commitment to rectify all the lives that they may touch in the course of their work. Most, however, hope that their work will start a positive movement that will increase like the widening ripples in a pool. Usually this does happen in a family because children benefit and so do others in the person's circle. Possibly, this is part of the increasing acceptance by the public of psychological counseling, for it is now deemed acceptable, even advisable, to seek such help. This results in more demand for services, and consequently therapists need constantly to consider what will be the most rapid and effective course of treatment.

These are among the reasons that there is great value and efficacy in returning to the source of the adult patient's learned attitudes. To include the original childhood family members in the therapeutic process is an effective means for the adult patient to resolve old family conflicts and to gain new perceptions of his relationship to that original family. He can experience new emotional interactions that can heal and redirect old disturbing self-appraisals and views about others. There is a good deal of reassurance in finding out that things need not always be the same, that change is possible in everyone. In fact, the usual message to the patient in therapy is that he is the one who has to do all the changing. Here then is a proposal that may mean changes on everyone's part, including parents, siblings, wives, and other relatives in treatment.

By adult patients, I mean a person approximately twenty to fifty years of age who has been living independently of his childhood family and who views himself as a graduate from the family nest, both emotionally and economically. Some people achieve this earlier than others. Not an inconsiderable number of individuals leave home at seventeen or eighteen and become self-supporting and self-directing persons. Occasionally one meets a person who made the transition at fifteen or sixteen, but this is now comparatively rare in our society. I am also talking about adult patients who are running their lives fairly adequately and who might not be any different from others who live on your block or occupy an apartment in your apartment complex. These people would be deemed neurotic, or as having some hang-ups. For the most part, they hold jobs of varying degrees of importance and are considered average citizens. They are distinguished probably by the fact that they decided to seek outside assistance for their marriage or for improvement of their personal life situation. This discussion is not aimed at treatment of schizophrenics or very severely disturbed people, although I have frequently treated such persons by similar involvement of older parents. Rather, the intention is to point out that using family systems ideas to assist average functioning adult citizens is appropriate and effective.

The original childhood family still has an important investment in the health and productivity of its adult members. They can be invited to participate in the treatment of the patient. If early experiences were harmful or inhibiting to the patient, they might not realize it but, when informed, would like to see what can be done to correct or ameliorate the situation. Older parents look back on their life perspective, which often shows them that in various crises they did not do as well by their children as they would have liked. They are now able to compare the way they raised their children with the way others did, and particularly, they now view it with new information about child rearing, which is widely available. They also want to feel that nothing is irrevocable and that their participation and help can be effective today, that they are not negligible in the lives of their adult children.

Further, the perceptions of the patient about how his parents felt about him and what they wanted of him is based upon a series of incidents. These accumulated incidents may add up, for example, to a highly critical attitude toward the patient. But why were the parents doing this? The patient feels that they just didn't like him, or that he was a born failure. In fact, there are often misunderstandings at the bottom of it all. Some critical piece of knowledge was never in the patient's awareness.

Case Example

Paula, a depressed young woman of twenty-six, was beset by feelings of unworthiness. Paula based this negative evaluation of herself on her mother's lack of attention to her as a child and the fact that mother often seemed to cry when Paula came home from school. Convinced that she was unlovable and a drag on the family, Paula withdrew more and more, so that communication became minimal and they passed each other almost as strangers in the house. Now, Paula was on her own, married, and with one child, but still feeling that she didn't matter much to anyone. Her mother kept in contact with her, but Paula made sure to limit the face-to-face contacts to just a few visits a year. As Paula clarified the origins of her feelings of unworthiness while in treatment, she saw that it was because her mother appeared inattentive, and seemingly disliked her so much that she cried when Paula returned home.

This appeared questionable to me so I asked to see the mother with the daughter. Mother said that the time that Paula described was a very crucial one for her. Mother was ill and finances were in desperate shape. She was so preoccupied with her troubles that yes, she did pay little attention to Paula. She often cried about her situation, but tried to conceal it, and was apt to be most tearful while Paula was at school. As things improved in the family, mother tried to reestablish contact with Paula, but was baffled by Paula's uncommunicativeness and reserve. In turn, the mother began to conclude that Paula did not like her.

When Paula told her mother about her early views of their relationship and the conclusions she had drawn about mother's behavior, mother was absolutely dumfounded. It had never occurred to her that Paula could interpret her behavior as she did. This situation was quite evidently based on a misunderstanding and continued by poor communication.

Older parents are frequently aware that they are on poor terms with their adult children. Seldom do they have the ability to talk directly to their children about it. It is too touchy a subject, too much like a loaded gun that might go off and kill someone. Better to keep quiet and hang on rather than risk an open break. Some do attempt it, but the adult child usually hears their approach as a complaint, a whine, or a demand, and so shuts off any discussion.

When older parents have reached their fifties and sixties, a dramatic change has occurred in the dependency relationship between them and their children. The children, while young, had been completely dependent on the parents and this continued until they reached their majority and went out on their own. Even then they may have relied to some extent on the parents for money loans, advice, or occasional baby-sitting. As time went on, however, the adult children were more and more leading their own lives, and their children (the grandchildren) were maturing and becoming independently active. The original parents, however, have grown older and are usually less active and have a more restricted circle of friends. Being part of an active family now becomes very important to them. They are considerably dependent on their adult children for a sense of belonging and continuity. The roles have been reversed.

Surprisingly, the adult children seldom realize this in a feeling way. Intellectually they know that their parents are separate and distinct from them and that they themselves, the adult children, are self-operating. Emotionally, however, they still feel that the parents have an upper hand in some way, just as they did when they were young children. For this reason, many adult patients resist the suggestion of including their parents in therapy. This shift in dependency relationships is valuable in two ways. It usually ensures the willingness of older parents to participate in the therapy of their adult child. From the adult child's point of view, he feels more self-confident about his ability to hold his own and confront the parents if necessary.

One often hears the old saw "you can't teach an old dog new tricks." This has not been my experience with older parent–adult child therapy experiences. Old dogs may not find it really worthwhile to roll over or sit up for a dog biscuit. But older parents find it vitally worthwhile to feel close and at ease with their adult children. That human drive for being wanted, for belonging and sharing, motivates them strongly to try new ways of talking or of not talking, to tone down irritating habits, or to limit expression of pet themes and peeves. They open their minds to new kinds of relationships that they might share with their adult children. It is possible to coexist with diametrically opposed views, be they political, religious, social, disciplinary, etc., so long as parent and adult child have agreed not to insist on the other's submission or compliance. They agree not to agree in a mutually tolerant way. All kinds of behavior can be refashioned via the goodwill and frankness engendered in such parent–child negotiations. Not that all would become smooth and frictionless. Certain personality traits may always remain as irritants, but they are less upsetting if certain kinds of behavior are frankly stated to be troublesome and are agreed upon to be avoided or soft-pedaled if possible. Also, it is true that many such traits are peripheral to the new contractual agreement to find some common interactional ground.

Including the original family is therefore of benefit to the adult child and to the older parent. Further, it speeds up the process of resolving many personal difficulties, because it does not have to be managed by third parties, such as therapists and fellow group members, but can be dealt with directly at its source. *Family* is a powerful word. It denotes strong feelings, strong attachments. I suggest that this power be utilized.

3

Patient, Parent, and Therapist Attitudes toward Conjoint Meetings

Some case descriptions will be given to illustrate the depth of the family's meaning, the intensity of attachment, and the pervasiveness of early childhood experiences and "training" for the adult child; also how family meaning and attachment can be used to improve the life situation of both adult child and parent. There are practical procedures and emotional attitudes that must be dealt with and many of these are included in a later chapter on procedures. Among others, these are: arrangements for meetings, patient's refusals, time required, strategies for handling typical family situations, follow-up work with the patient, follow-up contacts with the parent, and rigidities on the part of parent and child.

Before one can fully understand and appreciate the content and process of a meeting, there are two aspects of the encounter among adult child, parent, and therapist that need to be described. One is the attitudes and expectations of the adult child, primarily negative, who approaches a situation that routinely has been unhappy or destructive for him. The other is the stance and interventions of the therapist, which are often more active and direct (as well as directive) than in ordinary individual or family therapy. These factors follow in brief detail as a preface to the case presentations.

Preparing for the Meetings

The first question that will occur to many is what to do when the parents are dead or only one parent is alive. When both parents are dead, there are usually some relatives available who were in close contact with the childhood family and who can give information about early events. They also have some perceptions about the personality functioning of the parents, although the actual motivations of the parents in such events are usually based on surmises. These relatives also are usually interested in keeping in contact with the adult child and are concerned about his welfare.

In the case of an only child, very often there are uncles and aunts who knew the parents at the time the child was growing up. Since people generally try to maintain blood ties, one finds that the adult patient can call upon these relatives. When there are brothers and sisters, these relatives can be included. Normally, the older siblings are of more assistance because their memories go back further than those of the adult patients. Again, the odds are that the adult patient has kept in touch with his brothers and sisters, although sometimes those bonds are quite tenuous. Siblings have, in my experience, been quite willing to join in the discussions about parent–child reactions and sibling-to-sibling reactions, and have given really valuable information and assistance that leads to new insights about what was going to in the patient's learning experiences.

When one parent is still living, he or she can be involved. The relationship of the parents is now important to consider. Those who were openly feuding before one spouse died are usually more frank about what the difficulties were, and about the family relationships. A certain proportion will withdraw and invoke "you shouldn't speak ill of the dead." This is usually a defensive maneuver intended to keep some parts of the family history secret. Such secrets are not too flattering to the surviving spouse or are open areas of contention with the adult child. Most, however, try to give as accurate an assessment as they can of the deceased spouse's actions and point of view, and their own reaction to them. The desire for closer relationships with their adult child is usually stronger than any notions of gallantry or reticence about past unsuccessful relationships.

Those who would like to keep a "hearts and flowers" aura about the past, however, may also do this because it is their way of dealing with people and events. In such cases, it is useful to obtain information from other family members, such as brothers and sisters, or uncles and aunts. Sometimes it is necessary to include such another family member in joint sessions to jog the memory of a surviving parent, or to present factual material to bring about a more realistic focus.

There seems to be little difference between the problems encountered by an adult child with a foster parent or adoptive parent and those involving the child and a blood parent. Child and parent have perceived their roles in essentially the same way in each case. The foster parents with whom I have met seem to have been just as deeply involved with the child as if they had been blood parents. This held true even when the foster parents had undertaken the parenting job without official responsibility. Whenever a relationship was important to the foster child, meeting with the foster parents could be a means of improvement in the lives of both parties. This is what did happen.

The above discussion has been directed toward situations that took place in the past and that have left their imprint upon the adult patient. Here we might also discuss the inclusion of parents who are making a distinct impact upon the independent adult patient in the present. There are interfering parents who overload grandchildren with presents against the parent's request; grandparents who show marked partiality for one child; grandparents who lecture children about their behavior, trying to instill in them Victorian primness and Lord Fauntleroy manners. Therapists usually hear about these family tussles in great detail and urge parents (the adult patient) to speak their mind and to negotiate some new arrangement with the grandparents. Therapists very seldom invite the grandparents, especially those who live some distance away, to join the adult children in attempts to straighten out these difficulties between them over grandchildren. I found joint counseling sessions to have generally been highly successful. This procedure will be discussed in greater detail later.

Timing of Introduction of the Idea

It is difficult to state the exact time when it is optimum to introduce the idea that parents of adult children should be included in the therapeutic process. In past years, I generally waited until the situation was sufficiently clear to indicate that help from the parents was needed and would be beneficial. In recent years, however, a short time after the preliminary diagnosis is made (perhaps even during the first or second interview), I now mention that the parents of the adult patient might be included. This is intended to serve as a sort of early warning and to give the patient time enough to consider the idea. At other times, months may go by without my raising the question of parents, because frequently patients do not really know what their difficulty is. Depressed patients feel a general oppression in all areas of their life. As they begin to disentangle the experiences that led them to have certain views about themselves and to have a hopeless orientation toward the outer world, it becomes clear that these ideas were obtained via childhood incidents.

In general, patients are inclined to believe that the past is rigidified and that they are stuck with their perceptions about themselves and the difficulties that ensue from those perceptions. They are also inclined to feel that there is a rigid and settled relationship between themselves and their parents, that nothing is going to be altered there, and that their parents will continue being the same kind of persons, making the same kind of moves that they have for years. When the question is raised about actually inquiring whether a change could be made in the parent–child relationship, most patients scoff at the idea as quite unlikely. However, they do see that it would be of value to investigate why a parent, for example, was always critical or always demanding, and that it would be valuable to know why their mother, for example, never counteracted the father's harsh discipline. The therapist first intrigues the patient's interest as to what was going on that caused his parents to behave in such a fashion. This is followed up by the suggestion that perhaps the relationship could be changed and that here is a chance to see what the patient can achieve in the way of exerting himself psychologically as an independent power, a chance to utilize clear communication and see whether a better outcome would be the result. It is also to evaluate whether he is really as helpless as he feels he is within the child–parent combine.

It has been my experience that the standard reaction to this suggestion is always met with a decisive negative from the patient. In fact, no patient during all of the years of my experience with this modality has ever responded favorably. At this point, I would be suspicious of anyone who embraced the idea immediately. The reasons that patients give to refuse and refute this idea are essentially the same. First of all, they consider that there is a long psychological separation between themselves and their parents;

that their parents are at one end of the continuum and themselves at another and that no change is likely. In fact, many say positively that no change can possibly be made. Secondly, the patient looks back at his childhood from a long historical perspective. He places his parents not only in another generation but almost in another age. It is like thinking of turning time back, as in science fiction time machines. Another very frequent reason for refusal is an overt and distinct fear on the part of the patient. This is expressed in such phrases as "absolutely not," "why that's the craziest idea I ever heard of, they're totally hopeless," "oh, I couldn't do that, it would be a terrible mess," "I wouldn't want to hurt them, and odds are they'd hurt me."

There also may be a transference problem involved when the issue of bringing older parents is brought up comparatively early in the contact, when the patient may not feel completely sure about the therapist's regard for him. It is probably based more upon a feeling that there is going to be an adversary situation that will make him, the adult patient, look as though he is merely complaining, or as though his complaint is not justified. When the suggestion is brought up much later in the treatment process, when the patient knows his therapist well and is relying upon him, there has often been the suggestion that if parents came in and told their side of the story, the therapist would somehow begin to believe them and desert the adult patient. It is seldom that the patient seems to feel that the therapist could be a club who would beat the parents into line. Although logically this might seem probable as an initial feeling on the part of the patient, in actuality it does not seem to occur this way. Considering these reactions, transference may be at the bottom of such resistance.

In those cases where there has been a very bad relationship between the older parent and the adult patient, it is often wise to wait until three criteria have been fully satisfied. The first criterion would be the development of trust in the therapist so that the patient feels quite sure that he will not be let down by the therapist and that, if need be, he will be protected by the therapist. The patient in such situations feels that the therapist has really committed himself to be a friend and a helper to the patient, and that he will not be dissuaded by any moves by the older parent. With a number of deeply disturbed patients, this situation of trust, of course, takes quite a bit of time as well as testing. The second criterion should be that patient and therapist have very clearly discussed what they jointly feel is the etiology of the patient's difficulty. They should be in agreement that certain well-defined problems arose within the childhood experience with the older parent and may also be existing in today's context. With such clear understanding of the particular kinds of hassles between parent and child, the meeting is clearly focused on talking over these hassles and investigating why they came about, how the parent feels about them, and what the parent and child can jointly do to improve the situation.

The third criterion, and an extremely important one, is a clear understanding on the part of the patient that conferences of this kind can be unpredictable. There is always the possibility that the older parent may choose to reject the patient, rather than to make any moves that may be different or may be conciliatory in any way toward the patient. One must recognize that many older persons have an investment in maintaining their ideas and their behavior, and if that is challenged, their whole identity may be challenged. In such a case they may find it necessary to choose between their view of their identity and their adult child. I have prepared for situations of this kind, therefore, cautioning the adult child that he must be prepared for a possible confrontation that will leave him with a parent who rejects him. The likelihood is considerably less that the patient will end the confrontation by rejecting the parent, and in practice this has almost never happened.

The possibility of the parent psychologically separating from his adult child is not very great. In my experience, it has occurred in possibly 5 percent of the cases, and then never within the joint interview itself. Such a denial of the parent–child relationship has usually occurred after a few more attempts on the part of both parent and child to get together. Nevertheless, it is a distinct possibility and it is only fair to the patient that he take it into consideration and decide whether he wants to go ahead just the same.

Let us return to one of the objections that the patient raises about including parents. He is very apt to say that his parents are now in their late fifties, sixties, or seventies and it is not very likely that they are willing to change any of their attitudes. I have dealt with parents up to the age of seventy-nine and have found that this does not mean they are incapable of taking a new view or incapable of wishing to bridge in some way the gap between themselves and their adult children. There are, as is true of most persons, differences in capacities, and seventy years are borne more lightly by some persons than thirty years are by others: Some seventy-year-olds still have inquiring and quite flexible minds. Age alone, therefore, does not preclude involving a parent. Adult patients often feel sorry for parents who are in their late years, and they aver that at the parents' time of life it is a shame to disturb them or to bring new troubles into their lives. It is my conviction, however, that families do wish to get along together and that if there is some opportunity for a better relationship, for a constructive change, the patient is not asking a detracting thing from his parent but rather is offering that parent the chance of something very warm and vital in life—the closeness of parent and child.

I have spoken of the resistance of patients to the inclusion of relatives. It is interesting to note that, with almost no exceptions, patients feel strongly that *none* of their relatives will be interested in joining such a meeting. One would think that patients would have more confidence that their brothers and sisters would be willing to come to such meetings, but here again the negative view is almost universal. Even with brothers and sisters who have made some moves toward intimacy and who have perhaps talked together about the common difficulties they have had and may still have with their parents, the adult patient feels that his siblings would like to remain out of it all. The possible exception to this resistance is the family friend, cousin, or uncle whom the patient may have been close to, and who often has assumed a semiparental role. Here the patient is apt to say, "Well, *maybe* Uncle John would really be willing to come."

This doubtful view of the willingness of parents and siblings to join in counseling is a measure of the separation and hurt that has plagued the patient throughout his life. It is a reflection of the many refusals, criticisms, and rejections that he feels he has received from these family members throughout all his life. It is not possible for the patient to look hopefully upon a new response from his relatives, and most of the time when he agrees to meet with these relatives, it is very much tongue in cheek. One often feels that in the back of his mind the one reason that he is going through with this procedure is his desire to show the therapist once and for all that the family is hopeless, and that his views of the whole thing have been right all along.

Personal statements from patients and parents who have experienced these meetings provide the most vivid and accurate picture of the process and outcome of the procedure. I have collected letters from individuals who have met together in these adult child–older parent joint working sessions. Such persons now look back at those experiences from the vantage point of time. Some of the letters concern recent experiences. Some of them describe joint meetings with parents and adult child that took place more than ten years ago, and yet their recollections are as vibrant and poignant as if they had had the meeting only yesterday.

With the authorization of the individuals involved, I will quote from some of the letters to illustrate part of the process of my technique. While the letters are from parents and from my patients, the adult child, I have included more from the adult child than from parents. I chose to do so because the therapist will have more responsibility and intimate contact with the adult child than with the parent. Consequently, the therapist needs to know the apprehensions as well as the timorous hopes for change and improvement that his patient usually experiences. I have appended fictitious names to the letters because I may refer later to the further process of these particular interviews and to the results of the confrontation. Those who are interested in the outcome of these individual cases can, therefore, correlate the names with descriptions of results. No names are used within the quotes so that the identification of the individuals is impossible.

The first group of quotes illustrates the most basic and pervasive feeling experienced by those who contemplate a direct confrontation, parent to child. It is fear. Although hope hovers in the background, there are apprehensions of dire results and emotional explosions, and fear of final, irrevocable separation. The letters also reflect the wistful, tentative hopes for improvement between parent and child.

Dear Lee,
When you first mentioned the idea of having my parents come out [from the southern United States] to talk with us, I was torn in many different directions. I wanted them to come out so that I could tell them off and get them out of my life and off of my back. Right behind that feeling was also the feeling of complete and total fear. I was petrified with the idea of telling them some of the things that we had been talking about. I really didn't think that I had the courage to confront them with the way that I viewed our relationship. I remember when you had me write the post card to them telling them that I wouldn't have time to write to them much anymore, so that they would know that something was going on. I was so scared that whole weekend to answer the telephone. Whenever it rang, I started shaking. Finally Sunday afternoon I had reached the conclusion that I was at least safe until Monday because they hadn't called yet. It was shortly after that that they did call. From that phone call on, what had really been in my mind, a hypothetical get-together with them, started to take form. The two desires, to get them off my back and

out of my life started to spiral upward with the fear of seeing them under these circumstances.

Picking them up at the airport was really difficult. It was a very long ride for all of us. We all knew that there would be a lot happening later on and it was like waiting for the starting gun for a race that you had no idea how to participate in and if you even really wanted to win in. At every turn in the race there could be a whole new set of rules, that nobody had told you about until you broke one of the rules. I know that I didn't get much sleep the night before and my folks said that they hadn't either. I knew that you would be in there on my side, but I also knew that I was going to have to summon up more courage on my own than I ever had in dealing with them. I was frightened yet somehow optimistic. At least I knew that whatever happened it would be over with by Sunday afternoon and that was something definitely to look forward to.

Regina

Dear Dr. Headley,

When you initially pointed out that mother's will continued to dominate my life, I was disgusted with the idea. It was ridiculous to think that a 34 year old male could be tied to his mother. As you elaborated, the idea made more sense. In our discussions, mother took on the role of monster, forcing her will upon her weak and unaware offspring. I was comfortable discussing the roles until you proposed that mother join the discussion. At that point panic set in. The monster would hear what had been said about her and maybe become angry or worse yet, hurt. I dismissed the idea of facing mother in our discussions thinking she would not come so far a distance to talk with me.

As plans were finalized, I was anxious and disgusted with myself for putting mother to so much bother. Prior to your first meeting, I read mother my autobiography[1] as I wanted to defend parts of it. Hours before we were all to meet I experienced relief because finally I would tell mother my thoughts, many of which conflicted with her ideas, but my thoughts had become very burdensome and she would share them with me. It was humiliating to talk about my desires of avoiding responsibility because I was admitting weakness to a very strong person.

In the days to follow our meetings, mother and I openly discussed past events and emotional bonds. Mother seemed to accept what she heard and wanted to work towards a solution to current problems. The problems had seemed insurmountable to me.

Peter

---

[1] I often ask patients to write their autobiography in order to shorten the process of history taking.

Here is an excerpt from a letter from John:

The idea of facing one's father in the psychologist's office is at first thought—frightening. How is he going to take it? Will he be angry? Will he make light of it? Will he even go? I felt the idea had merit because it helped my wife to see the futility of dealing with her parents in her way and to some extent it relieved her own feelings of guilt. Their reaction to her helped her to understand.

John

A letter from Martha:

Dear Dr. Headley,

I feel sure that you remember the three person session that we had—you, my mother and I—several years ago. Looking back at that meeting now, I see it as a quite decisive turning point from mother's point of view, as well as from my own. And I'd like to try to link some of the pieces together—the way I see it.

As I remember (rather dimly in some areas), I was deeply depressed and anxiety ridden to the point of almost total immobilization and really wanted to stay in bed all of the time. In desperation, I asked my mother to come to my house (she lives some 500 miles away in another city) and take care of me. She came, and not unwillingly. When she arrived I began to feel not so alone in the world, but within a day or two we had slipped firmly into the same fruitless bickering and arguments which had been a recurring pattern in our relationship since I had had my own home and she had had hers. When I angrily complained about this to you you suggested, to my shocked surprise, that the three of us get together and try to find out just what was going on right at that time. I remember protesting rather violently that it would do no good whatsoever as "no one had ever been able to do anything with her," or to stop that constant talking, talking, talking. However, you gently, calmly, and subtly prevailed, and mother (again, not unwillingly) agreed.

Parts of that meeting, I think, I don't recall at all, but other parts are electrically vivid. I remember your calmness and what seemed to be a general understanding on your part. I remember the sound of my mother's strident, insistent, acid voice going on and on and on. I remember myself sitting in a small armchair holding on to the arms with every ounce of strength in me. I was terrified, sweating, shaking from head to foot and for quite a while, unable to talk . . . to speak. I'm sure that much was said by all three of us, but I don't remember much clearly. (Perhaps you do—)

Martha

Dear Lee,

I must confess when the prospect of asking my parents to sit in on a therapy session was suggested, my response was negative. I felt very apprehensive for several reasons. One reason was I still didn't like to admit "publicly" (or really to myself) that we were undergoing therapy. It was a private matter, and although my parents were aware we were seeking help, I had not discussed it with them in any detail. Another reason for my apprehension was that I was afraid that by involving my parents in my problems, I would somehow alienate them. I could visualize them resenting somehow being held responsible for my inability to cope with my problems. Still another reason for my negative attitude was that I believed my parents felt I was a much more mature and competent person than I really was and I hated to destroy that belief.

Maryann

How does it benefit all concerned in a family to have some members come into a psychologist's office?

I was afraid of being disowned by everyone if I challenged them. I felt if I didn't toe the line as trained by my mother and a close friend of the family, people would disown me. After several months of office visits my brother was asked to come in, and he did care enough about me and the problems so he came in. As it was hard for him he was twenty minutes late, but much was achieved.

Tony

Who Will Take Charge of the Meeting

It is wise for the therapist to maintain control of the interview at all times. In view of the fact that both parents and child have little idea how to go about such a situation, it is well for the therapist to open the meeting. It is essential at this point to express one's appreciation of the parents for taking the effort, and to state the therapist's position that he has no preconceived notions of blame, nor is this to be a criticism session. Parents naturally come with some trepidation, and they rather expect to be found at fault. There is a great deal of material in the press, movies and TV that indicates it is the behavior of the parents that has made the individual sick. Consequently, parents come rather defensively, and often frightened, to the interview.

INTERVIEW [2]

THERAPIST: Barbara had told you, I know, that she has been very depressed and has been in therapy. She also tells me that in recent months she has not seen you very often, and that there have been some angry exchanges. I thought you probably were feeling puzzled and upset about this, and so I suggested to Barbara that you talk with us. I feel sure you want Barbara to be happy, and to be on good terms with you, and vice versa. I thought we might understand each other better and straighten some things out.

MOTHER: (Sadly) I suppose I made a lot of mistakes and I am responsible for her depression and her marital problems.

THERAPIST: I don't assume that that's the case. I figure that you tried hard to do your best by her, and maybe something went awry between you that you don't understand.

MOTHER: That's right, and I wish I knew. Anything you or Barbara can tell me, I'd appreciate. I do want to help her.

BARBARA: Is that so!? Then how come whenever I tell you about something bad that happened between Mel and me, you start telling me about some neighbor who had a similar problem and got over it because she prayed, or because she got into some charity work for others? You're just telling me that my troubles aren't so great. I don't have any guts, or I'd pray my way out or lose myself in do-gooding. You don't care about me. You only want to get rid of the

[2] In the following examples, short excerpts have been taken from the total interviews in order to illustrate particular techniques or problem situations.

unpleasantness of my having a problem or disturbing your life. OK, I won't disturb your life. I won't come around.

THERAPIST: Mrs. W., Barbara is pretty upset, as you can see. She has drawn a lot of conclusions about what you feel and think about her, but I am not so sure she's read you right. From your point of view, what's going on in you in an encounter like that?

MOTHER: It's true I said that, but I didn't mean she was wrong or gutless, and I don't want her to stop talking to me and visiting, but I just don't know what to do. I feel I've got to help her somehow, but if I just criticize Mel, that doesn't help. I had kind of the same problems in my marriage and didn't have anyone to talk to. I know how she feels.

THERAPIST: You mean your own parents and relatives weren't of any help to you?

MOTHER: Well, they implied I would just have to live through it.

THERAPIST: Then maybe you don't know how to offer the support and concern that Barbara wants.

MOTHER: No, I don't know what I should do.

BARBARA: Well, if you'd just listen and hear me out and show your interest and concern. A hug wouldn't hurt, and maybe saying, like you just did, that you know how I must feel. I didn't think you *did* know.

MOTHER: Yes, honey, I do, but it doesn't seem enough.

THERAPIST AND BARBARA: But it is!

BARBARA: I don't want you to solve my problems. I've got to do that myself in my own way, but I need to know you are there backing me, whatever course I take.

MOTHER: But, Barbara, of course I am. I guess I just didn't do it the right way. But now that we've talked it over, I feel better and I hope you will just tell me when I haven't said what you wanted. I'm not too old to learn.

THERAPIST: I'm sure you're not, Mrs. W. You just showed us.

DISCUSSION

This is an interview where the mother came at the daughter's request without a previous interview alone with the therapist. After the therapist had briefly outlined what the difficulties were, the mother immediately voiced her conviction that the therapist felt she was wrong. Here the therapist must immediately state that opinions are not fixed, and that there may be new understandings. If this is not handled immediately, the mother will go on thinking that there is little use of her saying anything. When the daughter accused her mother angrily of not caring, it was evident that Mrs. W. would not know what to say and would probably sit there and take the accusation and feel worse and worse. The therapist must immediately go back to finding out why the mother is not taking any action.

The mother, from her reference to her own childhood, had no instruction on how to be of help in problems that were not of such a practical nature that she could make practical adjustments. Many parents come from families where discussing problems was not the style, and such parents often are very good about practical things but of no assistance in matters of discussion or support. From this interview, it is evident that there will have to be many trials and exchanges between Barbara and her mother before they adopt a new course of action. The mother is willing, but she lacks the know-how.

One should quickly contain a typical kind of exchange in which parent and child start making accusations and contradictions.

INTERVIEW

THERAPIST: I am glad you could come to help us with Ted's problem. He has been very anxious and upset, and rather depressed and feeling under intense pressure. He worries about everything, particularly about his college work, and he is painfully overconscientious about all of his assignments. This is creating problems with his fiancee, who says he puts her last, and his studies first. He is always anxious and preoccupied whenever he is with her. For that matter, he is anxious and preoccupied when he is by himself or with anyone. Ted feels that he has to get A pluses and a B plus would be a failure to him. Was he always this way?

MOTHER: No, but his father definitely was, and kept after him all the time. Nothing less than superior and superb was allowable with him.

PATIENT: And to you, mother.

MOTHER: Me? I didn't feel that way.

PATIENT: But you never contradicted father, and went along with him. I never heard you ask him to lay off me. Now that he is gone, I have to perform for you. You want me to be a lawyer, and nothing else will do. No wonder I can't come and visit you. And be grilled about my grades?

MOTHER: But I never grilled you about grades.

PATIENT: Oh yes you do. How about last Saturday?

THERAPIST: Ted is convinced he has to prove to you that he is tops so you will approve of him. Let's go back to your never contradicting father, as Ted says. Was that what was happening at home?

MOTHER: I didn't dare contradict him. When the children were little and my husband started demanding perfect behavior of them, like a drill sergeant, I protested. I particularly fought with him once when he was hitting Ted. I tried to get the child away from him, but he knocked me down. I was unconscious for a while, and he paid no attention to me. When I came to and sat up, he told me that if I ever interfered again he would fix me.

THERAPIST: That must have been terrible for you. Did you have any relatives who could help?

MOTHER: No, they were all back East, and I had no skills to get a job so I could leave him.

PATIENT: I didn't know that happened to you. You always seemed jumpy and nervous and I was afraid to ask you anything. I just assumed you agreed with him.

MOTHER: Well, I didn't. I was relieved when he died. I am sorry you have ended up feeling we were both down on you. I want you to feel free and to do whatever you want. I don't think you have to be a lawyer. Whatever makes you happy is what I want.

PATIENT: Mmm. Sounds good, but I don't know if it's true. Sure doesn't fit in with the way I've felt.

MOTHER: But it is true.

THERAPIST: Ted, you have felt that your mother was demanding for a very long time. Maybe you will have to give her a chance to really tell you frequently how she feels. Perhaps from now on you should just ask her how she feels about some things, rather than assuming you know.

Discussion

In a situation where the patient shows hostility immediately, both he and the parent may turn to arguments and trivia, such as, did she grill him or not? Unless this is controlled, they will argue about times and dates and who was where to prove their point, and they will get away from an effective kind of communication and the real central difficulties. The patient is reluctant to give up his anger, and when the mother says that he can lead his life the way he wants to, he is reluctant to say quickly and unequivocally that he believes her. The therapist here injects a suggestion of the methodology whereby both can test out whether mother really is or is not controlling him.

In Ted's case, the patient's wife, who was quite friendly with the mother, was included in the parent–child interviews. Subsequently, a sister and a brother met conjointly with Ted and the mother, and relationships between the family members was much improved. Ted's former extreme hostility to his mother was replaced by a very positive attitude.

The therapist needs to have in mind two points continuously. The first concerns what might have motivated the original behavior; the second recognizes that there is going to be a joint effort to change established relationships. It is well to imply that nothing can be changed instantly, but that with continued effort, parent and child can make the necessary adjustments. Parents are often reluctant to continue to make further negotiations if they are met with a blast of hostility from their adult child. On the other hand, the adult child has had a long experience of unfortunate events, which makes him considerably resentful. He does not want to let go of his resentment immediately because it seems too shallow a transaction. Furthermore, he is usually fairly suspicious and does not want to take at face value some seemingly superagreeable statement by the older parent. It is well to stress that relearning can take place over a period of time, that changes need to be lived through in order to seem real.

4

Inclusion of Parents in Marital Therapy

Marital partners, whether legal or not, commonly fight over each other's behavior, which they read as sabotage of their individual goals and standards for participating in a marriage. This may be overemphasis on material possessions, work, or activities that take away from family involvement so that there is no feeling of genuine togetherness. Many wives complain about "workaholic" husbands. These husbands come from all walks of life; they need not be professional men who stay at the office on Saturdays and evenings. They may be laboring men or blue-collar workers who always have some extra project going, preferably outside of the house. The counterpart of the workaholic husband is the wife totally devoted to her children's activities, at home, at school, or in their various other involvements. The husband feels just as shut out as the workaholic's wife.

Bitter warfare between spouses over discipline of the children leads many to seek marital counseling. When parents clash over discipline, they usually are fighting about fundamental philosophies of child training or marital obligations. These ideas are mostly absorbed from their own childhood families, or the spouse is feeling upset about parallel experiences in his or her own childhood. One parent may be overly harsh in discipline, to which the other parent responds by being too easy in discipline in an attempt to even out the program for the children. The result is constant conflict between the spouses, and frequently the children manage to utilize for their own purposes the differences in opinion between the parents. Each spouse feels betrayed in his parenting, betrayed in the marital contract, and put down as a person. All three aspects—parent, spouse, person—have been learned through the childhood family, either as a duplicate or as an opposition model. While most people have also absorbed other data from reading and discussion, it is the basic emotional "set" that is likely to prevail in actual performance.

Excessive emotional dependency of one marital partner on the other causes pervasive friction. This can be the wife who expects her husband to be totally wrapped up in her as in a continual courtship. She may expect him to manage and direct all affairs of their joint living. More frequently, however, it has to do with a more subterranean kind of dependency in which the husband is so emotionally dependent on his wife that she often uses the description "It's just like having another child in the house."

Perhaps less troublesome, but also encountered, is the spouse whose emphasis is on material possessions and pursuits rather than on sharing a relationship. The fights focus on money but they are about relationships—which one's goals are more important, or how the use of money proves one spouse doesn't care about the other's feelings. Lack of sharing lies at the bottom of two other problems. One is the husband or wife who is completely self-centered in style of living, and the other is the spouse who resists participating in social life. These persons lead a very restricted life within the home and usually force the partner into similar isolation because of their dependency.

A fair number of people with marital problems come to a

therapist because one member of the family is distraught about something going on between the spouses and the other person refuses to talk about it. This leaves the other spouse in a position of either having to swallow his anger, smash dishes, or take it out on the kids. The latter frequently happens, so that a child's problem soon is discovered to be really a marital problem. Inability to express emotions or anger makes it impossible to discuss and negotiate solutions to a problem. Such an inability is usually the result of living in a family where the parents had concealed from the children any differences they might have had. This might have been due to following an earlier psychological edict that it was very traumatic to quarrel in front of your children and that this might mark them for future unhappiness.

The facts of the matter are that when children have no opportunity to see how adults can disagree, argue about the disagreements, and then come to some mutually satisfactory conclusion about the matter, they have lost any instruction as to how to accomplish such a thing. At present, there is a great deal of material published and otherwise disseminated about the necessity to learn how to fight. Fight training, as it is called, is a common course available through psychological clinics or often through adult education courses. At this point it has almost become a format complete with standardized moves and equipment. For this reason, I will not cite a case example of this kind because such examples must be very common at this point.

Therapists now are often consulted by wives whose husbands are unable to show emotion. He is the facts-and-figures man, the reasonable person, the one who looks somewhat superciliously upon the other's emotional outbursts. The usual concomitant of this inability to emote is noncommittal behavior, lack of affection, lack of complimenting, and frequently the substitution of sex for affection and relationship. As a rule, those persons with the inability to show emotion grew up in childhood families in which the message was clearly given that getting emotional was going to upset somebody. They were trained not to make any trenchant observations about what they felt, positive or negative. The negative feelings might be too close to the truth and would arouse somebody's anger or sorrow, or there might possibly be a retribution. The positive feelings were often not responded to and were not encouraged.

Sexual functioning is now the subject of much attention. Besides factual information, there is a wide spectrum of books dealing with the attitudes that spouses should take toward sexual activity—from submission of wives to husbands, to "open marriage" philosophies. The latter is often interpreted by one partner or the other as a sanction for sexual encounters outside of the marital dyad. Thus it is possible to buttress one's existing philosophy or actions on the basis of these newly popularized books. In most sexual incompatibilities, however, the basic problem is a faltering personal relationship between the two partners. Couples disagree on the behavior expected in a marital situation as well as behavior and attitudes that the partners have as people; the disagreements result in frigidity, sexual affairs, and increasing impotency.

Many of these frictions in the marriage are based upon individual personality problems that preceded the marriage. Those in turn originated in the childhood family where attitudes were absorbed about male–female relationships. Marital problems are thus based upon these old dysfunctional family models and poor present interrelationships.

As one listens to these expressions of partners' woes, it is clear that ideals of married life have shifted from previously prescribed roles. The nuclear family of today is striving toward an equality between participants, and the ideal is for a close, communicating, emotionally exchanging family. The economic base is also shifting. Thirty percent of married women in this country are working. This probably accelerates the trend toward equal sharing of responsibilities by spouses. More husbands want wives to share with them their interests, conversations, and recreation. Wives want to be recognized as persons in their own individual style, their feelings respected, their ideas solicited. It is due to this striving toward partnership that sexual complaints, as well as others, boil down to expressions of perceived relationships: "You don't care about me and your behavior shows it" or "You think that you're better than I am and that's why you treat me the way you do."

Two generations ago, husbands were the main disciplinarians. Wives now complain that husbands don't take a large enough share of discipline of the children. They feel it should be a day-to-day affair with fathers noticing what's going on with the children and sharing with wives what corrective action should be taken. Wives are also asking that husbands and fathers show tenderness, give emotional support, show and verbalize their own feelings. A considerable number of men are unable to do this because of inherited-by-learning ideas about marriages and children. One way of breaking through the habit pattern is to meet jointly with the parent or parents of the husband to establish a more effective and significant emotional relationship, first with the parent and then, by extension, with the present family.

Case Example

Jim and Susie had been married for thirteen years. They now had two children, and Susie was exceedingly frustrated because Jim always gave factual answers to her emotional appeals to him, either about her or the children's needs or about the children's behavior. He tended to look blankly at her if she became annoyed, making no response to her remarks or angry behavior, remaining silent, and refusing to respond in any way. He seemed to turn off her comments without any visible distress or even irritation.

Susie was left with no outlets, except banging doors and shouting at the dog, or snapping at the children. She was really infuriated when Jim's co-workers would tell her what a "nice guy" he was and how well he listened to them. Fairly soon in the joint interviews Jim and Susie described his parents as turn-off experts themselves. They had a standard set of evasive procedures into which they launched whenever anyone asked a question of them that might require an exposé of some emotional attitude. Jim and Susie were unanimous in feeling that the mother was unapproachable and nominated father, who was sixty-seven, as the most hopeful alternative. We debated whether Susie should be included in the interview, since her relationships with father were positive. It was decided not to do so since father might be too threatened.

INTERVIEW

THERAPIST: Mr. Grimm, has Jim explained to you what we want to do and what it's all about?

FATHER: Yes, he said he and Susie are having some rough times and that she says he never shows he loves her or pays attention to what she says or feels. I think he's kind of like me. It's hard for me to say exactly how I feel. Never seems to come out right. I don't know how I can help.

JIM: Well, why don't we at least try to understand each other a little better.

FATHER: Well, sure.

THERAPIST: Jim means, I know, that he not only wants to learn how to show his feelings to Susie, but he also wants to feel closer to you.

FATHER: Oh, well, I'd like that, but I don't know how to go about it.

THERAPIST: Well, there are some past things that Jim would like to talk over and try to understand how you feel

Inclusion of Parents in Marital Therapy

about them, or felt about them. Then there are some present things that he'd like to bring up.

JIM: I guess the past things would be easier. Dad, do you remember when Mother had her breakdown? She went to the mental hospital and Aunt Flo moved in to keep house. Nobody ever said what was the matter, and when I asked, people shut me off. I asked again only a few years ago, and both you and mother said, "It's all in the past, it's all over and done with." End of discussion. Now it seems to me that I felt pretty confused those days about it. Still am. Something was going on. Somebody must have been feeling bad. What about it?

DAD: (Looking very serious) You remember that you had a sister that didn't live. Well, mother was sick after that baby came and the baby was sick too. We went to a lot of doctors, ran up a lot of bills. We were poor then. Your mother was in one hospital and the baby in another. I was working at two jobs trying to keep our heads above water. Then the little hospital where the baby was called me to say the baby had died. I went up there and picked up the baby's body, bought a child's coffin for it, and brought the baby back in the coffin to the cemetery. That was the worst day in my life. (The father had been looking sadder and began looking down at his hands as he told this. There were tears in his eyes as he said the last sentence. The therapist leaned over and took his hand. The father gave a tremulous smile in return.)

JIM: (Looking uneasy) But wasn't there anyone to help? You felt bad.

FATHER: Flo was sympathetic, but I had a sick wife and kids and bills, so I just went back to work. The baby's death made your mother worse.

JIM: Wow, dad. I'm sure sorry. You won't talk about it because it still hurts you, huh?

FATHER: Yes, it was awful, but we all get over these things.

THERAPIST: One does, but the most valuable thing is that you were willing to show Jim today that you can expose your true feelings.

JIM: I appreciate it.

FATHER: What about these present things?

JIM: Well, there's something I'm upset about. You always talk about me to your friends, or anybody, as Judge Grimm, and you introduce Susie as Judge Grimm's wife. I have asked you not to do so, but you keep doing it. Everybody knows I am a lawyer. You don't have to tell them, but it's as though you didn't hear me or I don't matter.

FATHER: But, I am proud of you.

JIM: It sounds like your pride in me is more important than that we get along.

FATHER: I see what you mean now. I never thought about that. You want me to stop it, right? You're just Jim?

JIM: That's what I want. Then there's another thing. All this discussion about finances and who's worth what, and how much you have put in the bank for the kids, but I'd rather you just talked to the kids and heard about their school activities or something.

FATHER: I guess you'll have to remind me on that one. Maybe you could poke me. I sure don't want to have bad feelings between us.

JIM: Neither do I. That's why we've got to hash these things out. Now, there's something else I want to talk to you about.

DISCUSSION

Therapist starts by checking what Jim has told father. He may have made it so vague that father really didn't understand it. Father responds well but says he doubts that he can do anything. Jim is irritated and pushes. Therapist reminds father what he stands to gain. Father might well overlook this. Then as the past events are recounted, father shows far more emotion about the baby's death than Jim had thought possible. Jim, however, does not know what to do about his father's emotion. Therapist shows concern by manner and touching. Jim becomes bolder and brings up the present problems. Father agrees readily as he understands Jim's feelings. Jim then goes on to other frictions and makes some new arrangements. They both feel that the joint interview was quite successful, and Jim later includes a brother in such a joint session to talk about their relationship.

This was one family where the wife of the adult patient might have been included. In general, it is not advisable because it may dilute the intensity of parent–child transaction. In addition, the spouse can deflect the discussion or help the other spouse avoid direct expression. This was a restricted father, and his son had the same traits. They did not become immediately close and confidential, nor did they eventually become intimate. Personality patterns were too well set in both of them. However, they did communicate more directly and were able to negotiate better arrangements between them. They arranged to spend time together in a more profitable way than had been true in the past when they saw each other.

Jim became a more emotionally expressive person in his own home. He responded to Susie when she was angry as well as when she just wanted to discuss her feeling about the two of them or the children. He was considerably more able to take self-assertive action, both positive and negative. The marriage was reported by both to be stronger and more mutually satisfying.

A letter follows from a parent who was asked to participate in conjoint sessions concerning her daughter's marital difficulties. The letter speaks for herself and her husband, the father, who also came.

> Regarding involving the family as a whole in marital problems, I feel the experience with my daughter and son-in-law's problems was, on the whole, a very worthwhile thing. It gave us a better insight into our daughter's emotional problems. Also a more intimate peek into her husband's personality and his problems.
>
> However, it did create a tremendous mental anguish for my husband and myself at the beginning. We were completely unaware of any deep-seated resentments against us. At the present time relationships between us are good. Involving us did clear the air of many misunderstandings and I feel if problems do develop, we are more capable of handling them in a more constructive way which would not be possible had we not been included in the picture. Our love of our daughter is in no way less and perhaps has increased (if such a thing is possible!) At least we try and show it more. The understanding of her and her husband and their problems is better.
>
> Mrs. J. T.

Marital Problem: Extramarital Affairs

The origins of much behavior, including extramarital affairs, are complex and sometimes difficult to understand. The following is an example of a child–parent encounter over such a problem.

CASE EXAMPLE

Charles and Loretta were a young professional couple that everyone thought to have the ideal marriage. Charles was successful, energetic, and handy around the house, and they had a good social life. Loretta was attractive, vivacious, friendly, a superb cook, a good housekeeper, very supportive of Charles. Charles was the kingpin in the home. Loretta enjoyed doing special things for him.

Into this halcyon bliss came a bombshell. Charles had fallen in love with a married woman and was debating about leaving—now or after the other woman had divorced her husband. After he told Loretta, Charles became acutely depressed because he felt confused about himself and guilty about Loretta. Loretta came unglued. She cried constantly, couldn't sleep, was intensely anxious, and couldn't do her work.

Individual and joint interviews elicited the following information. Loretta's family experiences had made her into a mother substitute, a self-punishing woman who concentrated on doing for others. She was a very dependent wife, although an independent businesswoman. Charles came from a family in which the mother appeared to control the family, not overtly, but through strength of personality and a husband who was passive. The parents always seemed self-sufficient and in seeming agreement with one another. This was Charles's stepfather, a man whom Charles respected, but had little knowledge about. There was an older brother, who from the age of six had lived with the real father. There seemed to be some family mystery involved.

Then Charles's mother died rather suddenly. Charles and Loretta went to the mother's home immediately. Loretta reported that neither Charles nor his stepfather cried at any time. They went about the arrangements in a factual way. The stepfather seemed all right at first, but then gradually, after six months, slipped into a deep depression and stopped all social life. He went to work, came home, and went nowhere with anyone.

Charles described his meeting with Samantha, the other woman. It was two years after his mother's death. For about the last year and a half he had been having dates with other women, but these were not long enough to call romances—only brief affairs. He had increasingly begun to feel as though he was losing his bearings, wasn't sure what he wanted to do, was in some indistinct sort of turmoil. The affairs seemed to give him a temporary feeling of certainty and worthiness. When he met Samantha, it was almost *déjà vu*. She was what he wanted, positive, independent, well controlled, with a mind of her own, competent. Their romance was rather helter-skelter in view of their respective spouses. Samantha lived some distance away, so they got together for weekends. Still, Charles felt uncomfortable about Loretta. She gave him six months to make up his mind and choose between her and Samantha.

Meanwhile, he started to work very seriously in therapy. This produced two central discoveries. One was his irritation at Loretta's dependency and her willingness to do anything he wanted, which seemed to him like lack of self-respect. He had been despotic and he disliked himself for it. Secondly, he realized how dependent on his mother he had been. It was partially because of his stepfather's uncommunicative behavior, which caused him to lean emotionally on his mother. Partially, it was also an anxiety about his security with mother because the older brother had been left out of the family. It seemed strange because his mother was always taking on people's troubles. Since the mystery about William, the brother, seemed important, we decided to ask the father to join us. Charles wanted to know about the parents' relationship so he could understand some of his own behavior. The stepfather had an important job in his company so it was a while before he could arrange time off; also, he lived in another state. Father arranged to fly to the son's home for a five-day stay.

INTERVIEW

CHARLES: As I told you over the phone, Dad, Loretta and I are separated. I think a lot of it is my problem. You and I have never talked very much and never about what we thought or felt about the family, just political discussions. I was surprised when you got depressed after Mom's death. You both seemed so self-sufficient.

FATHER: It was a big adjustment for me. Seemed I didn't have anything to count on anymore.

Inclusion of Parents in Marital Therapy

CHARLES: She was a strong woman and I really didn't realize you depended on her so much. Maybe I depended on her too, more than I thought. I have been thinking I'd like to know you better too. We've always been friendly, but not really close.

FATHER: You're all I've got left! Just ask me anything. Anything I can do—

CHARLES: Well, why didn't you let me know that she was really sick? It was only a few days before she died that you called me and said to come, that it was serious.

FATHER: Well, I just kept thinking she would be OK. I guess I really never believed she was seriously sick.

THERAPIST: Did the doctors keep you advised of her contition?

FATHER: Well, yes, but she never complained much. I never seemed to worry.

CHARLES: Now I wish it had all been more open, more discussion.

FATHER: Well, I'm sorry about that. I guess I just couldn't.

THERAPIST: Charles has had a strong reaction to her death, more than he realized. We need some information about William. Charles is uncertain about what happened there. As I understand it, William and Charles came with her when you two married, after her divorce, then William was sent to his father after a few months. Charles is puzzled about that, especially since William seldom visited after that, and only returned one time to stay when he was on leave in the service. You and he did not get along, Charles remembers.

FATHER: Your father, Charles, was too self-centered. He drank and gambled and ran up a lot of bills, always was playing the big shot on other people's money.

CHARLES: Up to the time of his death, from what I hear from some of the relatives. I haven't seen him more than three times since I grew up, but that makes it all the more puzzling why mother would let William go when she was aware of all of his faults.

FATHER: Well, Al gave her a bad time. Said he would go to court and all. Also, we were a little strained for money at that time. Then William was kind of sassy and kept saying he wanted to live with his dad who would give him lots of things. I found it pretty irritating.

THERAPIST: William was only six at that time, wasn't he, and Charles was a baby?

FATHER: Yes, that's right. So, Zelma decided to let William go with his father. I guess he had kind of a rough time with Al.

CHARLES: Yes, he told me so once when I went over to see him. I feel kind of guilty that I came out better than he did.

THERAPIST: So you can see that Charles got kind of shaky realizing that mother had made a decision that was very serious in William's life, and she could make a similar decision in his life.

FATHER: Yes, I can see where that might affect him. I always tried to fill in as the father. But Charles, I don't understand what is wrong between you and Loretta.

CHARLES: Well, we have some differences of opinion.

THERAPIST: Charles, you are avoiding the crux of the matter. How can your father understand without that?

CHARLES: Well, I have been having an affair with another woman.

FATHER: (Totally shocked) You didn't tell me that before. (Charles looks at therapist.)

THERAPIST: I thought you had told him, otherwise it wouldn't make sense to him.

FATHER: You are both such great people. I think Loretta is tops. I can't understand it (Shakes head).

THERAPIST: Are you angry at Charles?

FATHER: No, just shook. I, myself, would never do anything like that.

CHARLES: I'm not proud of it, but this is just why I need to figure out where I got my ideas when I was growing up. Besides, you and I have to start talking more to the point if I am going to straighten this out. I am grateful to you for being a father to me, but I think you should have told me about mother's illness, and I don't think you should avoid all your friends now. Also, I think we owe something to William and I intend to see him and see if we can't become better acquainted, closer together.

FATHER: Well, it's important to me to help, because I want to see you and Loretta stay together if you can.

DISCUSSION

Father and Charles then decide to meet the next day to work on some other facets of their relationship.

Charles determines that his stepfather was really dependent on his mother, that his guess was correct. The father won't really focus on mother's illness, so therapist moves to William's removal from the home. It is clear that mother and stepfather took the least difficult way out of the Al/William problem. Father is either not aware of any ambivalence on mother's part or doesn't want to face it. Clearly, Charles had a basis for a lingering anxiety about being kept in the family. Characteristically, he did not clearly tell his father about his affair and, when forced to do so by the therapist, finds father not condemning, but certainly reevaluating his picture of Charles. Charles then becomes more forthright in what he wants to achieve with father and brother.

From this series of interviews with father, Charles began to cool off the romance. He began to feel maybe it wasn't what he wanted. He then progressed to feeling that Samantha might not be a good match for him. She withdrew and returned to her husband. Charles began to reappraise Loretta, who had become more self-confident and more self-reliant in the course of her therapy. Within the year they had reconstituted their marriage on the basis of new rules and relationships. Charles may well have fallen in love with Samantha because she was so like his mother and provided the continuity of his dependence upon his mother. In contrast, Loretta had just added to his anxieties, for he felt her dependence upon him as a psychological burden.

5
Inclusion of Parents in Adult Individual Therapy

From the foregoing discussion on marital problems, one can see that marital conflict usually comes from the fact that one or both partners have individual problems. These personal difficulties adversely affect the ability of the couple to work successfully together as a team. Usually, the personality problems that underly marital hassles are also manifest in relationships and behavior outside the marriage.

Of the individual adult problems that come to the attention of the therapist, there are frequently patients who complain of depression but really have little idea of why they are depressed. Often they are depressed because of repressed anger or frustrated dependency, which results in feelings of helplessness. Such persons form a considerable bulk of those patients who are on the therapist's work load. There is another considerable group of difficulties that have to do with fear of people and inability to talk to others, or the inability to reveal feelings to other persons. This leads either to isolation or to superficial relationships, which the patient is well aware are far from satisfactory. Among women, many find themselves continuously hurt and in despair because of their own self-punishing behavior, which leads them to marry the wrong kind of man or to be put upon by various persons in their lives.

Many anxious patients are beset by feelings of unworthiness and incapacity to deal with whatever situation may arise. Those overcompensating for similar feelings are overly critical and hostile and are always at odds with their employers or those with whom they come in contact, which leads to referral for therapy. Spouses complain about obsessive-compulsive partners who are perfectionists, not only in their own actions but in the demanding of similar perfection on the part of others. Many identity problems arise with persons who are really not certain of their own worth or their directions in life, even of their own masculinity or femininity. A persistent group, and one that is difficult to treat, is the group of persons with infantile dependencies who have to be pushed and shoved to keep working for themselves and who frequently tend to cling to relatives, spouse, family, and therapist through many maneuvers, all of which are self-defeating.

The example that follows illustrates some of the ways that the adult difficulties can be dealt with via older parent–adult child family therapy to improve the individual's self-esteem and ability to take constructive action in dealing with others.

Case Example—Depression

Robert was a forty-year-old man who was referred for depression and also a tendency to be preoccupied with his health. He reported that he had been depressed most of his life but could not quite put his finger on the cause of it. One thing was clear, and that is that Robert was supersensitive to criticism of any kind, and in fact he could find a critical element in almost any transaction between himself and another. He reacted to this by long, rambling self-justifications and occasional real outbursts of anger as he told of the incidents. His work history had been erratic. He generally felt the men in charge of the job were critical, unfair, and demanding. This led to frequent changes of jobs and in some cases to altercations with the boss before he quit. His personal life was not very successful, either. The women he became interested in were not suitable, and he tended to vacillate in attentions. Usually this became irksome after a while and the girl friend either broke it off or Robert felt there wasn't enough going on there, so he would drift away. Robert seemed very vague about what was really at the bottom of this. It was decided to see if his family, who lived within a hundred miles, could be successfully included. Robert did not feel that either his father or his mother would come. Therapist first talked to his sister.

She was considerably younger than Robert and could not vouch for the circumstances when he was young, but said that in her opinion her father had always been a dictatorial man. He was precise and punctilious and demanded that everything be just so at home. Things had to be in their proper places, meals had to be served at exact times, conversations were to be brief and devoid of slang. When anything displeased him, he had a sharp tongue. Sister felt that Robert, an only son, had been more harshly dealt with than the sisters. She agreed with Robert that father was a respected, but feared, man and was not apt to agree to come to a joint session.

Therapist then talked alone with the mother. Mother reported the father's personality to be approximately the same as described by the sister. When asked why she did not oppose or temper any of this behavior, she said that she had tried to do so, but with little success. When she remonstrated with him for having sharply criticized Robert, father would glare at her, then get up and walk out of the room. He would refuse to speak to her for the next three days. The whole family knew that when father left the room in one of these episodes, silence and discomfort would reign for days. Father had a heart condition, which worsened when Robert was a small child. Mother was both afraid of father's anger and afraid that a really prolonged confrontation would cause a fatal heart attack. She was a mild-mannered, timid woman who was well thought of in the community for her charitable work. She agreed without much enthusiasm and considerable trepidation to come to a joint interview.

Therapist talked with the father, who had agreed to come to the joint sessions. Sister also was to be present because the therapist felt the mother needed some support and protection.

Interview

(Father is a man of seventy-five, thin, neat, perfectly groomed, and smiling. He leans on a cane. Mother looks apprehensive.)

THERAPIST: Mr. and Mrs. M. and Erica, thanks for coming. Robert and I have been trying to overcome his depression. A good deal of it is based on his sensitivity to criticism, which makes him feel very bad about himself, and then he gets to feeling blue and hopeless. Some of it comes from past experiences, but some of it has to do with today. Robert says he is reluctant to visit at home because he feels that you, father, are critical of what he says, and you, mother, do not respond to what he says to you with much more than "Oh, is that so," or he says you change the subject. I emphasize that this is the way Robert sees it. How do you see it?

FATHER: I think Robert sometimes makes statements without thinking it through, or without enough information. Now I do a lot of reading and I am pretty well informed about things, so I try to correct his misstatements. People should try to stick to the facts and not go off onto wild generalities. Lots of harm has been done in this country by ill-considered remarks.

ROBERT: But I am never right about anything as far as you are concerned, am I?

FATHER: Robert, I think that is an unfair statement. There are lots of things that you have done that are very good.

ROBERT: Well, let's see now. You remember when I was painting the garage for you a few years ago. I know how to paint. I've done it often enough, but you came out to look at it, and sure enough, there were too many brush strokes showing and the corners weren't well done enough, and I hadn't put enough turpentine in the paint. Do you remember that?

FATHER: Yes, I remember. Well, you should do your best on any job, no matter how small, and you've got to admit that it left something to be desired.

ERICA: That sounds like criticism to me, dad. Not a good job.

FATHER: (Angrily) No, it's not. It's just a fair evaluation of the situation.

SISTER: (to Mother) What do you think, Mother?

MOTHER: Well, maybe—(Father stands up, gathers his cane, and looks as though he intends to walk out.)

THERAPIST: Mr. M., if you walk out now, we will lose our chance of trying to get together as a family. I see you are angry, and that there is a difference of opinion here, but everyone is entitled to his own opinion.

ERICA: Yes, father, stay. You know this sort of thing happens at home when we don't agree on something, so it's always left up in the air. (Father reseats himself.)

THERAPIST: Thank you for sticking it out, Mr. M. I begin to think that you find it very necessary for you and the others around you to do things just right or otherwise you become uncomfortable. Is that so?

FATHER: Yes it is. It concerns me very much and makes me very unhappy if things aren't really well done.

THERAPIST: Perhaps when you see some imperfection in Robert, for there is imperfection in all of us, it's not so much that you were mad at him or disgusted with him as that you, yourself, are experiencing substantial discomfort.

FATHER: Well, yes, I guess that's a better way of putting it than I did.

ROBERT: Mmm. That's a new idea.

ERICA: I think Robert needs to have some real support from us, verbally, I mean. Sometimes maybe I haven't paid as much attention to that as I should. Robert, I want you to know that I think you have seemed much happier and more talkative lately. We have had some pretty good exchanges the last few times I've seen you.

ROBERT: Thanks, Erica. I felt that way too, but I didn't know that you did. It's a habit in our family not to say lots of good things we feel about each other. Dad, I was glad you came today. (Father smiles slightly, but makes no comment.)

THERAPIST: (To Mother) I mentioned that Robert often feels you don't respond to him. How does it seem to you?

MOTHER: Well, Robert often seems to say about the same thing over and over. Like how depressed he feels and how bad it is that he can't say what he feels to people because they will make some downgrading remark to him. Then he says how tired he is, and hasn't enough energy to go do this thing or that thing that he would like to do. I've run out of things to say to him. Besides, it seems that none of my remarks in the past have seemed to help. Maybe I do just say mmm, or just nod.

THERAPIST: Robert, what do you want her to do?

ROBERT: Indicate she's heard what I said.

THERAPIST: Like how?

ROBERT: Oh, like "sorry that happened," or "what did you do then?" I *don't* want remarks like "the Lord will take care of it." That's fine for her, but not for me.

THERAPIST: (To Mother) What do you think of Robert's suggestion?

MOTHER: Well, that's not very hard to do.

ERICA: Robert is right about the religious remarks, Mother. I respect your faith, but I don't think it helps Robert or me when you say things like that.

THERAPIST: (To Mother) Any reactions?

MOTHER: Well, I guess I'll think about that some more.

THERAPIST: Let's talk now about how you would all like to arrange discussions when Erica or Robert come over to visit. (Meeting continues.)

DISCUSSION

From this brief excerpt from the interview, it is clear that father is very rigid and set in mind, but that he is a compulsive man who feels that he has to keep others' standards up for his own comfort. He really does not see it as criticism. When Erica supports her brother, father immediately reverts to his standard behavior to avoid further confrontation. He thus protects his own ideas and makes his displeasure clear. It is doubtful that he intentionally wishes to make the others feel guilty. It looks more as though he has to escape himself. When this is verbalized, Robert is surprised and has a new view of his relationship with his father. Erica is encouraged by father's remaining, so she makes a further move in Robert's direction.

During all this the mother has sat passively. Therapist doubts that Robert can approach her directly about their relationship, and so initiates this new direction. Mother describes her reaction to Robert's complaints, but typically lets it drop. Robert might well not become specific if the therapist does not prod. Mother still is not contributing much. It is evident that the therapist will have to direct the interactions among these three as it is not their way to so interact.

A subsequent joint meeting with mother and Robert makes it even clearer that mother finds it exceedingly difficult to give any sort of feedback to either the therapist or Robert. Thus, it becomes clearer to Robert that he is depressed because he represses his anger. Nowadays he represses it because it costs him a job or alienates people, but originally it was because the parents would not admit criticism or anger, and there was no way of adequately releasing anger in such an environment. Also, Robert sees why he so easily felt criticized, learning that it came from his experiences with a perfectionist father and a passive, noncommittal mother. The other reason for his depression is his frustrated dependency. It is too risky to depend on father and too unsatisfactory to depend on mother.

After these interviews, Robert made some substantial progress. He was less depressed, got into more activities that he really enjoyed, and was less inclined to anger. His personality had, however, been fairly badly affected by his early experiences, and he was doubtful that he could make a successful marriage. This was acceptable as long as he could effectively manage his life without prolonged debilitating depressions. The relationship between Robert and his father became less stressful. Robert and mother had a more open relationship since he now persisted in getting some answers or reactions from her. She seemed more able to do so now since the restrictions on discussions were much less evident in the home following the meetings.

CASE EXAMPLE: OVERSENSITIVITY TO CRITICISM

A common reason for entering psychotherapy has to do with feelings of unworthiness usually expressed as lack of self-confidence. Not feeling worthwhile leads to not acting positively in one's own behalf. It can mean taking jobs below one's capacities, putting up with poor treatment by others, poor social life, lurking feelings of depression, self-criticism, and a host of other difficulties. Any one of these difficulties may impel an unhappy person to start psychotherapy. Usually before very long the source of this lack of confidence and feeling of unworthiness is connected with the childhood family.

Attempts of friends or of spouses to encourage the person are not generally successful because the feelings have been there so long and were ingrained so early. A case example follows of returning to the source of the difficulties via older parent–adult child interviews.

Case Example

Raquel was irritable with her co-workers and most of the time felt that she was not appreciated. It seems to Raquel as though everyone else was considered clever or friendly or charming, but not Raquel. Most of the time when she went out with the people who worked in her department of the firm, she came home feeling blue, or she was angry at someone and determined to quit the job. The next day she would cancel that decision because someone had asked her out to lunch or in some way had been friendly. These up-and-down feelings were very exhausting. One of her energy-consuming habits was mental arguing. Someone made a remark to Raquel that she felt was a critical one. She would then stop talking on the job or answer in monosyllables, and all day she would feel desperately miserable. Much of her thinking during that time was absorbed in long imaginary discussions in which she spoke her mind to whomever she was mad at, and sharp exchanges took place. Sometimes she came out well in the imaginings. Lots of times it turned out badly for her. Meanwhile, Raquel was jumpy, couldn't sleep, and was developing an ulcer.

Raquel felt life was just a continuation of what had happened at home. She was very frequently at odds with her mother when growing up. She felt there was little attention for her and that she was disapproved of. She responded by being rebellious, going with people her mother did not think much of, and getting into trouble at school. This effectively upset her mother, to whom appearances and reputation of the family were very important. Raquel's brother, who was older than she was, seemed to have no difficulties with mother or anyone else. They were still congenial at the present time with much to talk about, and Raquel noted that mother visited him more frequently than she did her daughter. Brother Glenn seemed to have everything—social graces, happy disposition, and a mother who did more things for him than she did for Raquel. What Raquel concluded from all this was that she was not as good a person as her brother, her mother was unfair, and there was no possibility of improving anything because her mother wasn't willing to talk about any of it.

Raquel began to speak up more as she progressed in therapy. There were some open confrontations on the job in which she fared rather well. She stated her views and they were taken into consideration. The participants in these disagreements remained friendly with her and made it clear they thought she was both capable and likable, although touchy. As Raquel gained strength she began to think about working on her relationship with her mother to try to find out what had gone wrong between them. Her mother was quite apprehensive about the meeting and her husband (Raquel's stepfather) tended to encourage the resistance. The mother finally came, however. A short preliminary interview determined that she was really concerned about Raquel's physical and emotional problems, and that she was herself a nervous, tense person.

INTERVIEW

THERAPIST: Raquel, I've explained to your mother what we have been working on together and that she might help us significantly.

RAQUEL: You know, mother, I tried to talk to you about some of this and we didn't get very far.

MOTHER: Well, I know we haven't been getting along very well, but I don't know what you want me to do.

RAQUEL: It's probably more an attitude than anything else. Somehow I get the feeling from you that I'm always wrong. Now Glenn and you always get along so well. You are Johnny-on-the-spot for any times together with him but somehow when I ask you to come visit there's delays and maybes and it often ends up with your not coming. I feel as though it has always been that way.

MOTHER: You mean ever since you were a child?

RAQUEL: Yes. You know we didn't get along very well. You must remember that we were always fighting.

MOTHER: But that was when you were ten or eleven, not before. It was about the time I went to work. I tried my best to give both of you as much time and attention as I could. (Tears begin to brim over in her eyes.)

RAQUEL: Yes, it was about that time, and it wasn't very long after you married Dad [stepfather]. I felt you weren't very interested in me but you were in him and Glenn and the rest of the family.

MOTHER: I wasn't more interested in him. You were into trouble all the time and that's what we quarreled about, and we quarreled a lot. Your stepfather was unhappy about your behavior, as you know, and I didn't want your aunt and grandmother and the rest to know about it.

RAQUEL: That's a lot of it right there! You're a people-pleaser mother, and everything in the family should be smooth and happy, even if I'm not listened to. You think I'm wrong because I argue and get mad.

MOTHER: No, I don't. It's true I don't like arguments and I try to be fair to everyone.

RAQUEL: What about Glenn. Is that fair? What about you giving him those things of grandfather's that I asked you for?

MOTHER: I didn't give them to him and I don't remember your asking for them. I'll get them back if you want them.

THERAPIST: It seems Raquel is rather convinced you don't care much about her, starting way back after your marriage.

MOTHER: But I do love her! (Crying and going to Raquel) I want to do whatever I can for her! (Raquel receives her mother's embrace rather warily.)

THERAPIST: From that you have both said, it sounds as though two things happened at about the time you both started quarreling with each other. There was mother's marriage and her going to work. I wonder if you, Mrs. Z., became preoccupied in adjusting to a new marriage and having more responsibilities on the job and at home.

MOTHER: I remember it as a rather frantic time. Fortunately, Glenn was older and was occupied with his own activities. I may have paid less attention to Raquel than to him and to some of my close relatives including my mother, who was ill.

THERAPIST: What do you think of Raquel's statement that you are a people-pleaser?

MOTHER: It is true that it is very important to me that people like me and think well of me. I have a great many friends here from my job, and in the old neighborhood. I feel very unhappy if someone dislikes me or disapproves of me.

THERAPIST: Raquel is very alert to having people like her, too, only often she is uncertain about when the people really do like her. It may be that you two started growing apart as a result of circumstances—a new marriage, a new

Inclusion of Parents in Adult Individual Therapy 91

job, and a girl especially needing attention in such a new family situation. Now Raquel still has some of those needs. She would like you to pay attention to her opinions and disagreements with you, and talk about them openly. Would you be willing to do that?

MOTHER: Yes, I am. I'll do the best I can. If Raquel feels I spend more time with Glenn than I do with her, I certainly will make some arrangement with her as to how we will arrange it in the future. I wouldn't want her or anyone to feel that there is favoritism in the family. But I love Raquel and want to help.

Discussion

The meeting verified several feelings that Raquel had had about her mother. Mother needed to feel "right" about any situation, and so she found it hard to deal with disagreements. She evidently felt it necessary to feel secure by having everybody like her. To do so she would need to always be alert to opinions and needs of others out of the family. As is often the case, immediate family members were more taken for granted. Raquel's anxieties about being liked were logically acquired from her mother, both by example and by seeming to be ranked second to her brother. Mother, if she felt blamed for anything, was admittedly in considerable distress and became very tense. This prevented Raquel from following up grievances in a persistent manner because it was difficult to argue, and when she did she felt guilty about upsetting her mother. This was the basis for her anxiety, depression, and resistance to confronting anyone.

Mother did, however, have many loving and concerned feelings for Raquel. Following this session, mother became more attentive and willing to discuss any friction. The brother became solicitous and concerned also. He and Raquel became much closer and more confidential, at which point she discovered that he had his own personality problems, which resembled hers. The need to be liked, to appear well adjusted, and to have no problems or insecurities was a characteristic of mother, Raquel, and Glenn. Probably mother had been trained by her own childhood family in the same way.

Her new perceptions of the family, plus new behavior, helped Raquel to be more positive in her approaches and attitudes to other people, and less suspicious that they might have basically negative feelings about her. One noticed a marked sense of relaxation in regard to her mother and much less need to demand attention and approval. Her attitude toward Glenn slowly changed from resentment to sympathy and concern as they became more frank. She felt from those discussions that Glenn had been equally affected by mother's insecurities and by stepfather's reserved relationship.

I quote from two letters commenting on changes of feeling about self and family relationships following joint family meetings. They are from persons you already know—Maryann and Martha.

> *I saw myself as not having lived up to the ideals my parents had set for me (whatever they were)—although they seemed to be pleased that my husband is a professional man. I found myself in a very difficult time. With three small children, scheduling babysitters became a major undertaking. I never felt I could ask my mother for help. I became very resentful but could never express this to her.*
>
> *I'm afraid some of the details of the sessions have become hazy to me (it was some years ago). I do remember it was a tearful experience. However, I do remember that my mother hugged me after one of the sessions and told me she and my father would do anything they could to help. I began to feel that maybe I had misinterpreted their motives and expectations. On the contrary, they seemed proud of my accomplishments and rather stood in awe of how I was able to handle a very active household and a demanding social schedule. I found they were willing to help when they could, but they would be honest and tell me when it interfered with their plans.*
>
> *The relationship I now enjoy with my parents is relatively tension free. I feel I can approach them with my problems without fear of censure. My fa-*

ther has shown great willingness to offer his support. I feel that this relationship, based on the understanding of each other's feelings and expectations, is a direct outgrowth of the sessions we spent together in therapy. Those sessions certainly got us on the right track in communicating honestly with each other. For that, I shall always be grateful!

Maryann

The outcome of this confrontation in a controlled environment was, I think, quite clear to both mother and me in the area of the feelings involved. Being us, we didn't openly discuss it, but both of us behaved rather differently. Mother seemed less domineering, more willing to take some responsibility for herself, more able to interest herself in something without having to have my attention focused on her constantly. I felt less anxious, less needing, and less that she was going to engulf me as I stood there helpless to do anything about it. I think I hated her less and feared her less—at any rate, none of our old weapons seemed so necessary anymore.

Martha

6

Siblings Join in Therapy of the Adult Child

Interviews with siblings are of two sorts. Frequently, they develop out of joint interviews with older parents because material is brought out that concerns the sibling. At times, this is an overflow of feeling from the joint session, as the adult patient wishes to extend the circle of understanding and good relationships. Sometimes the parent and adult child would like to share their perceptions of events or their joint plans for implementing a new relationship. They would like to have some input from the sibling and to increase the viability of changed relationships in the family. For instance, in Ted's case, more historical material seemed necessary to understand why father found it so necessary to demand perfection and why the mother was so fearful and resourceless. As parent and adult child talk these things over, they naturally turn to the question of how it affected the other children. Sometimes the question arises as to what other relatives, like uncles, aunts, and cousins, felt about the family transactions, and how were they reacting to it. In Ted's case, both he and his mother expressed concern at the end of their first joint session for Lori, Ted's sister. She was married to a man who drank and who was intolerant of the children's behavior. Mother had not been able to approach this problem directly with Lori and, in fact, had scarcely been able to think clearly about it, because it seemed so much like the duplication of her own marriage. Ted had been reluctant to say anything to Lori because it seemed to him like interfering in their lives. From his own experiences, he was unwilling even to seem as if he were directing someone else's life. Mother and Ted decided to talk to Lori about their joint meeting, and to ask her to join them in a following meeting.

Family feelings are very powerful, and an improvement between two members is apt to set off a chain reaction. The change is sufficiently exciting and energizing that the original members of a joint session want to involve others and help them, as well as increase the scope of their goodwill and warmth. Often several siblings will thus be involved. It is particularly useful to have several joint meetings of this kind because the adult patient gains more experience each time in confronting and clearly communicating his thoughts and feelings. It also affords him an unparalleled opportunity for reality testing. He can offer new arrangements in place of those that have been confining or hurtful. He can present new facets of himself, sometimes aspects of his thinking and feeling that were discouraged by old family rules. *Hope* and *change* are allied words. One stimulates the other.

Another reason for joint meetings of siblings lies in the inability of either a parent or an adult child to meet jointly. Almost all the time it is the reluctance of the adult child to ask a parent to come, because he believes the parent won't come, is incapable of change, or will be too disturbed by the revelations of the adult child's difficulties. Essentially, it is the adult child's unwillingness to take a chance. There are a considerable number of such reluctant patients. One alternative is to invite a sibling to participate in a joint session. This will usually be very attractive to both siblings, and the outcome of such sessions is normally very beneficial.

An example of such a sibling joint session follows.

Case Example

Jack had come to a crisis in his marriage because he was no longer able to keep secret his several affairs. These had been going on for five years without his wife's knowledge because they were daytime assignations usually, and he was home at night. One of the girl friends became so persistent that the wife began to realize what was going on. After some time spent in denials, he admitted the extramarital affairs. The whole thing seemed to him as though he were two different people. He loved his wife and there were no sexual problems between them for the last five years, although there had been some previously. As he described the affairs, they seemed more like encounters in which he received a validation of himself as an interesting individual. Much of the time was spent in lengthy discussions about life, people's reactions, etc. He did not at any time envision leaving his wife. He genuinely did admire her for her abilities as a writer, her homemaking abilities, her social graces. In fact, he really did not have any serious complaints about her.

Work in therapy indicated that he had led a very restricted life in his childhood home, restricted in the sense that the goals and standards for behavior and thinking had been rigidly set and enforced by his parents. His father exalted hard work, accomplishment, and money. His mother valued religion, strict moral living, church attendance, status, and formal family contacts. Jack had really never talked to them about himself or his feelings. For one thing, they did not encourage it, and besides, if it fell outside the scope of religion or accomplishment, he felt they would not even comprehend him. The family had done well and he, as the successful son, was the pride of the family. The other four children had not done quite as well, however, and were a source of worry and concern to the parents. One son was unmarried at over thirty, another son had not been successful in a business venture, and a sister had had a difficult divorce. Jack began to feel that his affairs had been adolescent explorations into a life that had been off limits for him, and that his girl friends were attractive to him primarily because they were viewing him as an individual. He did not mention his family to them, or his accomplishments in the area of business or social status. As a matter of fact, he tried hard to keep these matters out of the focus of the relationship. Jack felt that his mother was completely unapproachable, and he would not ask her to come to a joint session. First of all, she could never forgive him for an affair. Secondly, he felt she would never be able to talk about any of her attitudes. He saw his father as equally rigid. Consequently, he asked his brother Al to join in the sessions. Al was very willing to come, and he was aware of Jack's extramarital affairs.

INTERVIEW

(Al entered rather nervously and immediately introduced himself with an account of his business address and activities.)

THERAPIST: Al, I'm not sure if Jack gave you some background of what we are trying to do.

AL: I know about Jack's affairs, and he's told me he is trying to figure it out.

THERAPIST: Did he mention that we feel that the family background has something to do with it?

AL: Yes, and I think so too. It screwed us all up. I never could understand why Jack was doing all this. Mom would have a fit if she knew. Maybe that's part of your reason, Jack.

JACK: I thought about that, but I'm not really conscious of any wish to hit back at her. It could be there, I don't deny that. What I think it's about is the crazy way we grew up. Mom stamping approval or disapproval of the girl friends we brought around. There were few of those though, you know.

AL: Yes, I know. You were always working, even when you were a kid, and then going to that boys' school didn't give you much opportunity. I think that's what Mom planned, to keep us so busy that we couldn't think about girls. Remember how she watched and worried whenever Cousin Rose was alone for five minutes with her boyfriend. Sex was such a bad thing, you couldn't even say the word. Remember how she bawled out Uncle Jake for telling an off-color story.

JACK: Yeh, I remember. Then there was that other time—

THERAPIST: Jack, is that another incident? I don't want to get too far off the track.

JACK: Yes, I guess it was. Al, has this family of ours affected your sex life and your life in general? I get the picture you don't feel too secure about yourself.

AL: Both, I think. I get turned off sexually by nice girls, the kind you marry, and I manage to ruin those relationships. Then I get turned on by the girls that mom wouldn't approve of, but I can't get serious about them because *I* don't approve of them either. So, here I am, over thirty, and I don't know if I can get married. I want to, though, but it seems not to work out. Now you are the shining light in the family, the successful one.

JACK: Huh, how can you say that. Look what I've just done to my wife and my marriage. Being successful in work is OK, I enjoy it, but that's not all there is. Look at you and me, this is the first time in our lives that we ever talked about ourselves, or how we felt about our family. That's not much to be proud of. Here you don't know me, and I don't know you. In fact, I don't even know myself, or I wouldn't have gotten in this mess.

AL: Well, we've got to get out. I've got to get this good girl–bad girl complex straightened out. I think you are in the same boat, and it's mostly due to Mom's clamping down on us.

JACK: Do you think she could ever change?

AL: No, impossible. Dad might listen, but I don't know about him either.

JACK: So it's up to us. At least you know what you feel more than I do.

AL: Yes, I'm ahead of you in that. Another thing I feel. We've got to help Joe [another brother]. He's all mixed up. Why don't we ask him to come here with us?

JACK: OK with me.

AL: This is the first step, talking to you like we were just people, without all that family obligation, ranking and all that. I'd like to spend time with you in some other way than we used to, those girlie places, just more normally. I don't even visit with your family much.

THERAPIST: Al, you seem to recognize that your family training mixed you up about sex and relationships. Have you ever talked to anyone about it?

AL: Not really. Who was there to talk to? I mean who was there to listen? Maybe Jack and I can straighten our heads out together.

THERAPIST: It's going to take more than just this get-together, I am sure of that. Also, it's going to take a reevaluation of what's really worthwhile to you. You both need to take a second look at your family's values.

Discussion

This part of the opening session with the two brothers was continued with several sessions, including the other sibling. Jack stopped all his extramarital affairs but was still very much overinvolved with his work. The other brothers really needed some continued individual work following the meeting with the older brother. This interview showed clearly the kind of competitiveness instilled in the family, and the negative view of sex by the mother.

There was one critical point in the interview when the two brothers might well have gotten off into comparing notes about their mutual experiences, which would have diluted their real talking about feelings and plans. They did draw closer together when they realized that they both had disabilities as a result of their family training. The expression of concern for each other was a very distinct break in the competitiveness. For Jack, it was a relief that he did not have to keep up the standard of success that was enforced by his family. It probably would have been more effective if the father had been asked to participate, as both Jack and Al felt that he was open to expression of feelings if given an opportunity. Perhaps the mother was as rigid and unyielding as they said. These prognostications have not always been right, in my experience.

This is a quote from Tony's letter about the outcome of his meeting with his brother. If you recall, he was very apprehensive about it and feared to be totally rejected.

> My brother learned there were some problems[1] that to him were very simple and part of life, but to me they were very serious and deep rooted. He will

---
[1] Severe social and personal inhibitions.

never know how serious they were to me. But the psychologist pointed out a few and asked him to respect my feelings in some of these matters. He didn't completely understand, but he did back off and later said, "Anytime you need to talk to me about problems between us, do so."

Finding I had some solid ground to stand on with him, I started to tell him off and let him know how I felt about every problem between us, and then stood my ground 90%, which is now closer to 100%, with fairness and some bitterness. It taught me that my brother didn't disown me and has taken a lot from me which is helping me to get along with him, and also be myself when I am with him, rather than how I should behave from my training when younger. As I got older, I could not stand the old regimented family ways.

7

Typical Transactions with Parents

There are some typical family transactions in which parents attempt to deal with their adult child under the old family rules. In most instances the family will establish new procedures. Occasionally, the parents show very little flexibility and in such cases the adult child may have to state his decision to act as an individual who recognizes but does not submit to the family system. Some examples follow.

The Good Old Days

Parents (or a parent) seek to smother all pertinent discussion by a flow of verbiage. The accounts of past events tend to be repetitious and the patient has usually heard it all before.

INTERVIEW

THERAPIST: Mr. and Mrs. L., as John was explaining to you, he seems to find it very difficult to be aware of other people's feelings. He doesn't seem to know when his wife is mad at him or when the kids are hurting because something unhappy went on at school.

JOHN: Yeh, I just seem to get stuck. I don't know what to say to them. It's as though everything is so superficial. The worst is, I don't even notice how they feel.

THERAPIST: John says he's been this way a long time. In fact, he can't remember anything particularly going on that was disturbing or unusual as he was growing up. Was it really all that smooth and problem-free?

FATHER: Oh well, just about like any other family. We had our ups and downs. Mother was pretty sick when John was small. Let's see. Wasn't that after we moved to the new house?

MOTHER: No, it was just before. You remember we were thinking of buying a car, and it was shall we get a new car or new house.

FATHER: Oh yes, I think you're right. I had just left that old job of mine at Smiths. . . . (Father here launches into a long, detailed story. Mother adding corrections or additions. Patient looks bored and lost.)

THERAPIST: Looks like you enjoy thinking of old times. Nowadays, though, John says he has a repetitive argument with you, Mr. L., about financial discussions. He says you lecture him about how he should invest his money. This makes him mad, because he wants to do it his own way.

FATHER: Well, I just want to help. After all, I've been in business a long time.

MOTHER: I hate those discussions. Takes up too much time, and you're both mad at the end of it.

THERAPIST: What would you like to see happen instead, Mrs. L.?

MOTHER: Well, John is grown up. Why can't he make his own mistakes?

THERAPIST: And you, John?

JOHN: Well, other people's ideas are useful, I suppose, but—

THERAPIST: John, I think you'd better be more direct. Tell your father what you would like him to do.

JOHN: Well, why don't we let it drop, all this business talk. We could talk gardening and sports.

FATHER: Well, I guess we could.

THERAPIST: Mr. L., I suppose you are trying to offer John something you feel you are good at. That's understandable, but John doesn't want it now. Could you agree to drop these discussions and try talking to John about some sports, or whatever else you think of, and see how it goes?

FATHER: Well, sure, I guess. We could try it.

THERAPIST: Great. Why don't we meet again in two weeks to see how that arrangement works.

Discussion

As the therapist brings up historical matters in an attempt to understand John's way of behaving, the parents avoid any real discussion, and if they were given their way, would continue to talk endlessly about the good old days. It is to be noted that John slides along with them and does not interrupt. The therapist might then pursue the family history by a series of questions about illnesses, changes, etc., but it appears from this early reaction of the parents that this would be time-consuming and not too profitable. Therefore, the therapist brings matters back to the present and some difficulties that the therapist knows exist between John and the father. Here there is a slight change, for mother breaks with the father and does not continue the game. The patient still would prefer not to have any confrontation but is forced to do so by the therapist.

Father is not very enthusiastic about suggestions made to him. However, when the therapist points out that he may have a good intention at the bottom of his behavior, the father is more willing to make an agreement to try a new style of communication. The odds are, however, that without some kind of continuing intervention on the part of the therapist, this whole family interchange could soon return to its sterility and surface exchanges. For this reason, the therapist serves notice that there is going to be some ongoing checkup to see whether the new system is really going to work.

The Bad Old Days

In this instance, parents wish to establish at once that they have suffered and struggled as parents, thus defining themselves as good parents. They also imply that it is unfair to them to question their loyalty or management of the family. The patient is immediately put on the defensive and seldom finds the strength to criticize such seemingly devoted parents.

This kind of reaction could be called "the bad old days." A case in point is Gino, a thirty-eight-year-old man, who had come for marital therapy because his wife complained that all he thought about was money and material possessions. Their house had to be spotless and "on show" all the time. The kids must look well dressed and have polished manners. Her friends were not sophisticated and upper class enough for him, he complained. He noticed and made derogatory remarks if her hair and makeup weren't perfect. He had a fancy new car, but she was unable to drive it for fear it would get dented. He worked long hours and usually on Saturdays. Meanwhile, no emotional exchange was going on between them.

INTERVIEW

THERAPIST: (To parents) Gino has just told you about the problems he and his wife are having. Gino himself isn't quite sure how he got to be the way he is. Everything seems kind of a blur to him up until his high school years, so we need some help from you about those earlier years.

FATHER: Sure seems funny that he's got problems now. Nice car, beautiful house, good job, healthy kids. Things were really different with us, I can tell you.

MOTHER: You see, we were depression parents. First it was welfare and living in some dump with rats in the garbage cans—in the house, too. The kids were bitten by them once. No clothes for school, except hand-me-downs from Salvation Army. Other kids used to tease Gino about his clothes.

FATHER: But we didn't stay down. I got a job and we moved. Then I got a better job, and we kept moving to better living quarters. In a way, it was kind of hard on the kids because we had to move them from school to school, right in the midst of the school year, but we wanted to do the best by them.

MOTHER: Then I got a part-time job so Gino could take violin lessons and ballroom dancing. You have to know music and dancing if you are going to go around with the right kind of girls. It really was hard, though. I just got back from my job when the kids got home from school, and then I had to start with housecleaning and cooking and overseeing homework.

FATHER: We did OK though. I got my first brand-new car when he was in sixth grade, a Pontiac.

MOTHER: He's been in business for himself now for quite a few years and doing very well, but it used to be terrible before that.

FATHER: Just ourselves to take care of now.

GINO: Would have been better if you hadn't had the four kids back in those days, wouldn't it? Lots less trouble.

FATHER: Well, you see we made it. I remember—

THERAPIST: You've described what you did in those years. How did you feel about being in that situation?

FATHER: Feel? Well, we did the best we could.

THERAPIST: There's no question but that you were hard-working and conscientious parents. Do you feel now that since you gave Gino, as well as the other kids, a good start that he ought not to be having difficulties?

FATHER: Well, I don't know as I'd say that. It would seem to me, though, that he has got just about everything.

THERAPIST: Maybe he hasn't had a chance to just share his thoughts and feelings of anxiety with you.

GINO: I've thought about telling you that Marge and I might separate. I've been kind of upset about it, but I think you might feel that maybe I'm failing in something.

MOTHER: Lots of people separate these days.

THERAPIST: You mean it wouldn't need to be a failure on Gino's part. Gino really needs your interest and concern now.

Discussion

It is evident that the parents are very much involved with their struggles and successes in their early married life. However, the struggles and the difficulties seem to loom larger in their memories than the successes do. They repeatedly point out that all of these terrible things that they went through were for the benefit of their children. For this reason, it is important to give the parents credit and to verbalize that they really were conscientious. However, it is more than obvious that given any chance, the parents would return to more accounts of their hard life. It was now natural to shift to a supposition that they might be slightly resentful that Gino had a more fortunate start in his marriage, even though that fortunate start was contributed to by them. Parents now shy away from expressing feelings, since this is obviously not their style. The therapist continues to emphasize feelings rather than facts, and Gino, for the first time, makes a step toward the parents, asking for their interest. Mother does not quite know how to reply but makes a roundabout statement that implies that Gino has done nothing wrong. The therapist uses this breakthrough from the mother, and from thereon would pursue the feelings of all three members of the family.

It's Father's Fault

Not infrequently the surviving parent who meets with his or her adult child puts the blame for the family dysfunction on a deceased parent.

Case Example

Mary, forty, had been unhappily married for sixteen years and had sought help from a previous therapist because of her anxiety and depression. She gained enough self-confidence to divorce her husband but continued to be depressed. She had originally married in haste to escape having to live with her mother when her father died. (She was an only child.) She and mother had been on strained terms all her life. She saw father as kindly and interested in her, and mother as demanding, critical, and hysterical. Mother had come from another state to help the patient through a particularly depressed period. In the first day they had had serious troubles. The therapist wanted to see mother anyway, as the patient claimed she couldn't express herself or be self-assertive in any way because mother didn't allow her to. The patient claimed that mother had made a companion-housekeeper out of her at an early age.

Interview

THERAPIST: Mrs. B., Mary tells me that you two are having problems in living together, even though it is a very temporary arrangement. (Mary, during this short speech, looks very frightened and shaking—a very different demeanor from any that the therapist has seen her exhibit so far.) (To Mary) That's it, isn't it?

Mary: (Still shaking) That's right, but there's no use talking to her.

Therapist: (To Mother) Mrs. B., specifically Mary tells me that you oversee every action of hers and correct it. Mary feels you want to control everything she does.

Mother: I do not want to control her. I have my ideas and she always opposes them. She wants everything to be done just so.

Therapist: Always? You mean that you feel that she has been opposing you for years?

Mother: Yes. Her father always sided with her, and if I ever complained, he said I was wrong. He was the one to control things. Everything was to be quiet when he came home. No one was to raise their voice, no noise, no disturbance. How can you have no disturbance with a child? But he threatened me again and again to break up the household if I couldn't keep things quiet and Mary happy. Oh, he chose her all right.

Patient: Oh, oh, how can you say that!

Mother: Because it's true. We were practically prisoners in the household. He didn't want my friends to come visiting at the house. It was too noisy, too much trouble, as though his executive job was that difficult! Why, he had been in that job for years before I met him. He was twenty years older than I was. My mother insisted I marry him—security she said—and he was young for one year—we went dancing and to the theater. Then she [Mary] came and everything settled down to routine.

Therapist: Did this make you feel Mary was a burden?

MOTHER: No, I wanted to be close to her, but he tried to influence her and separate us.

PATIENT: You didn't care for me. That's why you kept me so controlled.

MOTHER: No, it was him. If you weren't controlled, we would both have been out in the street.

THERAPIST: But now he's not here, so you don't have to control her, do you?

MOTHER: No, no I don't, and I don't want to. I want her to be free as I am now, but I still want to be myself around her. If we could just work something out.

THERAPIST: OK, then let's work out something about who's going to cook the meals, and who's going to decide what is to be cooked and how it is to be cooked.

Discussion

Very soon in the interview, mother puts the blame on father, and attributes all the actions that have not worked out well to him. There is no way that this can be disputed, since the patient apparently did not have any information about their relationship and there is no one else in the family who is sufficiently familiar with it. Mother explains all her actions of a negative sort as being under protest and being forced by the father. If allowed to, she will continue to give many evidences and incidents of how the father was essentially the controlling person in the family. From some of her reports, it does appear as though he was a much more negative influence than the patient had indicated from her information. The breakthrough in this interview comes when mother realizes that something needs to be done and expresses the desire for change. The patient is resisting, saying that you can't talk to her and, in general, she has negated the mother's comments. Therapist, therefore, picks up the mother's desire for change and starts on a very small tactical maneuver that will at least get them talking to one another and negotiating some settlement.

In order to illustrate some of the functions of the therapist, I quote some parts from patients' letters describing the process. Here is a quote from Regina.

I saw your participation in this situation as that of a protector. Before we all got together, I viewed you as being a buffer between my parents and I, so that they wouldn't just come in and bombard me. I wasn't going to be facing them alone. There would be somebody there that could rescue me when things got really sticky. After we got going I also saw you as an instrument for hearing and listening correctly. Trying to sort everything that was going on was really hard and I relied on you to be able to be somewhat away from the emotional aspect of the situation and to hear from an unbiased point of view what was being said so that a correct response could be elicited and made.

From Sam's letter:

I found that my relationship with my mother and father were at the root of my self identification and marital problems. My mother had passed away, so all I had left to work on was the relationship with my father. You suggested that I get my father to join me for a session in the office. When I first mentioned this to my father, he was very apprehensive. But finally he consented. I have learned that both my father and I have a great deal of difficulty in getting our emotions out in the open—perhaps my father even more so. You were able to bring to the surface the fact that I was in great need of my father's approval. Once he sat in on a session, you were able to make us see our emotional attachment to each other. You then pressed us to confront one another with these closely guarded emotions. Once out in the open, the three of us had a good crying hug. For me it was a deep, tension releasing, laughing cry.

I guess my father and I are making progress. Last week during a telephone conversation my father was able to tell me that he loved me and that he loved my wife. I have been able to do the same with him on several occasions. Being forced to face emotional realities and move away from pure "head trips" has allowed me to see how right this marriage is for me. I feel as though our relationship has had some obstacles removed and is growing strong and healthy. I guess this has shown that when people are willing to listen and change there is no limit to the growth that can take place.

Sam

Since Martha has a gift for expression, I would like to give you part of her description of the therapist's function:

What had started out as an early afternoon therapy session became the first direct confrontation with the reality of the situation in our lives—my mother's and mine. The sky didn't fall in, the earth didn't crack wide open, and nobody got crushed. This may have been the first confrontation for mother and me, but equally as important, it was the first time that either of us had had an ally—the first time that neither of us was alone in this dependency struggle. And you were the ally of both.

Martha

Martha has "hit the nail on the head." She has expressed the crux of the therapist's activity. Unless there is a genuine respect and caring for the welfare of both individuals, I do not feel that the outcome of these parent–adult child sessions is constructive. One must remember that parent and child are experiencing, often for the first time, a confrontation around the most basic of human needs—loving and sharing, and they are not prepared to explain it to one another. They need someone who will facilitate, but most of all someone with empathic caring who will share in and guide the strong emotions so rife in these meetings.

It's Grandfather's (Grandmother's) Fault

A variant on the theme that it is somebody else's fault is the parent who says his life was circumscribed by *his* parents, and that's the explanation for his behavior.

CASE EXAMPLE

Larry and Francine were in the midst of acute marital hassles. Among other problems, they fought over discipline of the children. Francine was for firm discipline and training the children to neatness, good table manners, and prompt compliance with either school requirements or parental direction. Larry could be approached by the kids and would let them go to the movies, out to play, etc., when Francine had said no. When Francine scolded a child, Larry was apt to go into the child's room later and take a cookie or say they had been there long enough, now go out and play. Naturally, Francine was furious at this undermining of her authority. Larry and Mr. W. are meeting because Mr. W. has visited frequently in the home and has expressed his opinions, and Larry also wants the father there for other reasons.

INTERVIEW

THERAPIST: Mr. W., Larry and Francine have asked you to come today, I know, partially because you have lived so close to the family and were aware of the disputes between Larry and Francine about keeping the kids in line.

MR. W.: Yes, I know, and I was glad to come to see if I could help.

LARRY: I suppose you think I would let the kids do anything they liked.

MR. W.: Well, you don't keep after them very much.

LARRY: I suppose you want me to be just the way you were, hard-nosed, no explanations, hit 'em first and ask 'em later.

MR. W.: (Startled) Did I seem that way?

LARRY: Seemed and seem that way. I guess you know, it didn't help us to be any more friendly, nor is it helping our friendship any when you back Francine.

MR. W.: Well, if you think I am a disciplinarian, you should have known my father. He was brutal, knocked us around like tenpins. We were real scared of him, but we turned out pretty well. I toned it down a lot when I raised my family. Really tried to think about it. I know we all were allowed to get out of things, and my mother maneuvered around to get us out of a pickle. That caused bad feelings between them. So, I decided to discipline as I felt it necessary, knowing kids are apt to lie.

LARRY: You didn't think long enough. I determined I wouldn't be like you, all righteousness and no compassion. I'd rather have my kids like me than have them as Boy Scout models.

MR. W.: Well, I was only doing my best as I was taught to do. That's the only way you know how to be a parent.

THERAPIST: That's understandable, but now Larry says there are some bad feelings between you, at least on his part. What do you say to that?

MR. W.: I feel shook up about that, and what can I do?

LARRY: Stop feeling so righteous that you are better than Grandpa and have it all figured out.

THERAPIST: Will that make you feel that maybe he could listen?

LARRY: Well, I'd have to see some action first, before I believe it really, but, yes, if he could see my point of view, it would help.

MR. W.: The thing that upsets me is that you felt I wasn't interested. I tried to tone down my discipline from my father's style, but maybe I didn't add the listening because I didn't have it.

THERAPIST: You are listening now, so I think Larry has many things to say to you. Maybe he could stop being just the opposite of you, if you could find some middle ground to meet on.

MR. W.: I'm willing.

DISCUSSION

Mr. W. is a father who feels that he was much better than his own parents, and so excuses his behavior on the basis of (a) it was learned, and (b) it's better than the previous behavior. His son openly attacks him and says in effect this isn't good enough. Father then retreats again to say that he's done better than his own father. However, he sees the separation between himself and his son and makes a small change in the discussion by saying that maybe the interest wasn't demonstrated enough. The therapist cuts off the return to father's early training and brings it back to the here and now as to what father is really willing to do to assist Larry and himself to a better relationship.

This discussion is apt to lead to Larry defining himself in another way than just a diametrically opposed model to his father. It will, in any case allow him to include, perhaps, a few more disciplinary measures without feeling that he is duplicating his own father. This is a very common source of either overdisciplinary or underdisciplinary action on the part of parents. They see one facet of their own parents' behavior, which was hurtful to them, and consequently they throw out practically all of the parents' modelings in order not to be as disliked or as, in their minds, despicable a person.

I Don't Know What You Mean

This is a difficult type of transaction in which parents are immovable. It requires persistence and overt challenge by the patient and therapist.

CASE EXAMPLE

Beverly, a twenty-eight-year-old girl has had a series of engagements. She is reluctant to actually march down the wedding aisle, and so several suitors have departed after waiting around for some time in vain. Beverly is now becoming rather depressed and anxious. All her friends have been, or are, married. She concludes that there is something about marriage that frightens her. In the course of therapy, she realizes that the essence of her parents' marriage lies in the domination by the father of all phases of the family's life. In fact, her mother's personal choices and activities are dictated by her father. Beverly, herself, when she was at home was under her father's thumb. Beverly has tried unsuccessfully to talk to her mother about this. Finally, she feels that she cannot break out into full maturity until she has had some confrontation with her parents to speak about the family as she sees it.

INTERVIEW

THERAPIST: Mr. and Mrs. J., Beverly wanted to talk to you about her fears of getting married, and feels you can help.

MOTHER: We would like to. I can't understand it. She is so pretty and talented, and all the fellows like her.

BEVERLY: But, it is a big responsibility getting married. Look at you two. Mother, you always do what Dad wants.

MOTHER: I don't know what you mean.

BEVERLY: Take vacations. You hate the seashore. Dad loves it, and for thirty years, you have been going to the seashore.

FATHER: I don't get it. You mean we shouldn't go to the seashore?

BEVERLY: No, Dad, I mean why don't you ask mother where she wants to go.

FATHER: I do, and she says where do you want to go.

BEVERLY: Let's get to something else. Dad, you refuse to discuss anything, and we are never supposed to get angry. Usually what happens is I or mother would start to say, "I didn't like what you said," or "something you did annoyed us." We only get a few sentences out and then you say, "I don't want to hear anything more," and walk out of the room. Several times I have followed you, and mother has intervened and begged me not to. Why, mother?

MOTHER: Well, he has a heart condition and shouldn't get excited.

THERAPIST: Is that why you always agreed to what he says?

MOTHER: Well, one reason.

BEVERLY: Why couldn't you choose to go to the mountains with one of your friends?

MOTHER: Well, he always gets so upset over arguments and then he hates to be alone, so I go on the type of vacation he likes.

THERAPIST: That's quite a burden to always be carrying, Mrs. J.

BEVERLY: But don't you see I couldn't take on that kind of a responsibility for another person.

FATHER: I don't know what you mean. Isn't that what the marriage ceremony says—to go where you go, to cleave unto each other and something like that?

BEVERLY: But within reason!

MOTHER: What do you mean, dear?

THERAPIST: Beverly means that she wants to be a person with her own likes, dislikes, feelings, and perceptions. She means she doesn't want to be absorbed, but to share. (Both parents look upset and troubled. Mother keeps looking at father anxiously. He looks out the window. Beverly shrugs her shoulders.) It may seem like a very different way of thinking to you, but Beverly has formed some ideas about the kind of relationship she wants to have in her marriage. That way will not be your way. Do you think that you could accept that, even if you don't understand it?

BEVERLY: It's not that they don't understand. It's that they won't admit what's going on. Well, it's your lives, but I just can't keep on pretending that everything is OK at home. From now on, I am going to speak up.

THERAPIST: Looks like you have some new experiences ahead of you Mr. and Mrs. J., but Beverly's life is separate from yours and she will have to make her own way.

MOTHER: Well, I don't know—

FATHER: Mmm.

DISCUSSION

Parents rely early on their standard defenses of not understanding. They obviously feel unhappy about their way of relating and don't want it to be clearly revealed. Beverly tries hard to get through without success. The therapist speaks for her and supports her independence. Couples like this will not act as open individuals when seen together. When seen separately, or when interviewed separately with their adult child, they are more apt to make some sort of meaningful response to the therapist or to their adult child. However, there is not apt to be a great deal more. If any admissions made in such individual sessions are referred to later in a joint session, both will return to their "I don't know"s.

Martyrs

Martyrs are frustrating to deal with in joint sessions for obvious reasons.

CASE EXAMPLE

Jeanne, thirty-five years old, married, and with four children, became agitated and irritable after her parents decided to move to the same town in which she lived. They had been living in the South, with occasional visits on holidays. Jeanne had not gotten along with her mother for years and was on superficial terms with her father. The fights began to erupt between Jeanne and her husband; the children became hard to handle. Jeanne and Tom came for marital help, and in the course of it, it became clear that Jeanne had absorbed many things from her parents. Her mother was a martyr, and always managed to make Jeanne feel guilty about something. Also, Jeanne felt impelled to be supergood at things yet could not recognize her accomplishments when complimented for them. She was deeply suspicious about others, especially women. No matter how forthright the individual, no matter how long she had been a friend, Jeanne would pick out some spoken phrase, some absence, some behavior that proved she wasn't to be trusted. Jeanne became aware that these personality traits were the result of her experiences with her martyr mother, and her "hands-off policy" father. It was decided to ask mother to join us for a joint session because, along with everything else, mother was upsetting the children when they visited her.

INTERVIEW

THERAPIST: Thank you for coming today, Mrs. C. I hear you weren't too well this week.

MOTHER: Oh yes, I've had a return of my asthma. My doctor thought he would have to rush me to the hospital. You see, in 1945 I—

THERAPIST: Mrs. C., Jeanne would like to talk to you about some family things.

JEANNE: Yes, mother, I am getting upset because you buy so many presents for Tom [Jr.] and not so many for Jimmy. Jimmy's feelings are hurt. How come you're doing that?

MOTHER: Well, he's bigger than Jimmy and needs more things. Besides, he's the oldest. These are my only grandchildren and I would like to buy them nice things. We worked and slaved when you were growing up, Jeanne, and I feel bad that you didn't have more things.

JEANNE: Seems to me I had plenty of stuff. So, I do appreciate your wanting to please the kids, but I want it equal so the kids don't get jealous or fight.

MOTHER: Well, I'm sorry if I've done something wrong. It was really because they're my only grandchildren.

JEANNE: You mean that I am being hard on you and ungrateful.

MOTHER: Oh no, I didn't say that.

JEANNE: (Angrily) No, you didn't say that, but that's what you meant, and I know it. (Mother looks pitifully at therapist.)

THERAPIST: Well, regardless of what she did or didn't mean, the question is what can you two agree on. Jeanne, how would you like to have the presents arranged?

JEANNE: Well, two of the same thing if possible. Two games, or two balls, all about the same price and nothing fancy.

MOTHER: (Looking injured) Well, all right.

JEANNE: Can I count on that?

MOTHER: (Bridling) Didn't I just say so?

JEANNE: Yes, but I find you have several meanings to what you say. Like today, you said after I told you about my fun luncheon with Susie yesterday that you had been deathly ill all that afternoon. I think you meant what a selfish, ungrateful girl you are not to take care of your mother, didn't you?

MOTHER: (Whining) Well, I just told you about my afternoon after you told me about yours.

THERAPIST: I can see where Jeanne might read your remark as a criticism. It depends on the tone. However, I think, Jeanne, that you can ask your mother whether it was just an informational statement or whether it was a reproach.

JEANNE: Well, which is it, Ma?

MOTHER: Just information.

THERAPIST: So, we'll accept it at that.

JEANNE: Now this is just the sort of thing that goes on all the time and drives me up the wall. It's insinuations, insinuations.

THERAPIST: But we now have a means of determining what is statement and what is insinuation, or reproach. Isn't that what we just did, Mrs. C.?

MOTHER: Yes.

THERAPIST: Is it OK with you if you and Jeanne keep using this way to sort remarks out?

MOTHER: Sure.

THERAPIST: Then let's move on to the source of other frictions between you and ways of settling them.

DISCUSSION

In this interview mother first tries to say how sick she has always been, and in what a precarious situation she finds herself. The therapist cuts her off and returns to the present. Jeanne states her problem clearly, to which mother replies that she's just being a good grandmother, and puts herself down. Jeanne restates the message, but the therapist tries to get them to focus on a factual agreement of how things can be done. Jeanne then returns to the central problem that she has with her mother, that her mother makes her feel guilty. Jeanne makes it clear that she hears double messages from her mother. The mother denies this, and this could become a confrontation of "tis, tain't," but the therapist steps in and asks, or forces, the mother to choose one statement that she says is the real message. This leaves the two with a new agreed-upon *modus operandi*, and since the therapist has heard the agreement, Jeanne can always refer to it when she gets in a disagreement with her mother.

8

Hazardous Situations

The preceding case examples cover some of the typical situations. One that is not so common but that must be dealt with promptly is that of high, angry emotions. Here the therapist has to be quick and decisive.

CASE EXAMPLE

Sylvia was twenty-seven years old and had been working for some years in a job far below her capacities. She began to be depressed so that she could not concentrate well. Her boyfriends were fairly unsatisfactory, and she generally hung on too long to a failing relationship. Her general attitude was self-deprecating, and she almost felt grateful that somebody found her interesting enough to date her. As these relationships went along, Sylvia's boyfriends began to impose on her in some way, which eventually ended in a separation and hurt feelings.

Sylvia described her background as the Cinderella of the family, stuck between an older brother who seemed favored and indulged and a younger sister who was babied. Whenever a conflict arose between Sylvia and her younger sister, Dottie, the mother gave Dottie the toys or allowed her to have her friends stay over and not Sylvia's, etc.

Mother made excuses for Dottie in such hassles. "She was only trying to be equal to you, and really you are bigger than she is," etc. Sylvia withdrew more and more, leaving the family as soon as she possibly could. Father did not seem to join in these competitive games, but he was primarily interested in his job so that he was at home very seldom. Essentially, he was a silent, neutral figure. The older brother was no longer in the home, nor was Sylvia, but Dottie remained and was working.

Sylvia asked mother to come to see the therapist in a joint session to find out whether a better arrangement could be fostered between them. The therapist talked first with the mother to get some idea of her interest and capacities, since mother was reported to be laconic in the extreme. True, she was no talker, but she expressed her concern for Sylvia and said she wanted to help in any way she could.

INTERVIEW

THERAPIST: Mrs. D., I told Sylvia that we talked about the situation and that you are interested in helping.

MOTHER: (To Sylvia) Yes, I can see that you are depressed.

SYLVIA: Yes, things aren't going right for me. I split up with my last boyfriend. When that happens I feel lonely and am apt to come home to visit more often.

THERAPIST: Does it seem to help?

SYLVIA: Well, nobody seems to talk about anything directly at home. Nobody has asked me if I am sorry I broke up with Jim, or glad or what.

MOTHER: Well, you didn't mention much about it. I figured you didn't want to talk about it.

SYLVIA: But if you asked me if I wanted to talk about it, I probably would.

MOTHER: Do you want to talk about it now?

SYLVIA: No, I want to talk about something else that bothers me. When I was growing up I always felt that you would side with Dottie, not with me. The other night when I had that argument with Dottie, you stepped in and said she was right.

MOTHER: But, she *was* right. You are often too opinionated about things. You can't have everything your way. (Sylvia stares at her.) You're too much of a free thinker. Dottie seems to be erratic at times, but it's only youth.

SYLVIA: (Crying) So Dottie is always right.

MOTHER: (Angrily) I didn't say that.

Sylvia jumps up, her face flushed and her hands clenched. Mother also rises in a truculent manner, glowering. Therapist steps in between them and says to mother, "I think this is getting too out of hand for us. Will you wait in the waiting room for fifteen to twenty minutes while I finish talking with Sylvia?" Mother leaves. Sylvia collapses crying. Therapist's efforts are now to comfort her with Kleenex and an arm around her shoulder. Sylvia somewhat recovers. Therapist makes an appointment for the next day and Sylvia leaves by a separate exit from where the mother is waiting. Had the therapist not immediately intervened, the scene could have escalated rapidly. Neither party was hearing the other. The therapist brings mother back in. She is somewhat subdued, but still angry.

THERAPIST: What happened? I was surprised since you seemed so different from when we had talked before. Then you did not seem to feel that Dottie was more in the right in an altercation than was Sylvia.

MOTHER: Sylvia was attacking me, not Dottie. She has always been hard to reach, whereas Dottie is so agreeable and compliant.

THERAPIST: I am afraid Sylvia will be even more difficult to reach now. Sylvia's feelings have been deeply hurt. I am sorry it has happened. Maybe we'll have to let some time pass before your feelings and Sylvia's feelings settle down. It's clear now why Sylvia doesn't offer much at home. She's waiting to be asked about things.

Mother is still rather grumpy, so the interview is cut short. Notably, she expresses no regrets or concern about events. The discrepancy between what she said previously and her behavior at the joint interview indicates that she continues her nonhelpful attitude toward Sylvia and is not willing to talk about it further. Therapist then decides to see the father. He is more interested than mother but is not an outgoing or demonstrative man. He feels that providing for the family is his chief job. Unlike mother, he does not feel Dottie is "righter" than Sylvia. He sees the competition but is too placid to do much about it, except be friendlier to Sylvia.

(Note: In spite of the foregoing, this family did get along better together as time went on. Sylvia had made an impact.)

Discussion

This encounter illustrates a situation where the therapist must be very much in charge of the session. It is necessary to step in immediately to prevent any worsening of the situation, and at the same time try to salvage the relationship as much as possible. Both parties in such a confrontation are very upset. Sometimes it is best to have individual follow-up interviews with both as soon as possible. The immediate efforts of the therapist should be directed toward restoring calm, and to recognizing that each person has a right to his own views, no matter how divergent they may be.

Management of Emotional Scenes

I should like to comment here about management of emotional exchanges. It is quite possible for interviews to bog down in uncomfortable silence or withdrawal if participants do not recognize one another's emotional states. Very frequently, interviews between older parents and adult children become highly emotional. The participants are apt to break into tears as they describe their feelings about each other or about past situations. Since a great many of these families are not demonstrative, the individuals are apt to sit and stare at the one who is crying. The therapist then arises and goes to the person who is overcome by emotion, and shows by his action that the way to convey emotional support is by physical demonstration as well as by verbal sympathy. This often mobilizes the other family members to come to one another and offer their sympathy and concern.

This same kind of blockage occurs when something good happens between members of the family. If there is a breakthrough of some kind, and family members turn from being negative about someone in the group to being laudatory or to expressing a liking for them, they are still inclined to sit in their seats and make no demonstration of the feeling. Here the therapist may very well get up and take one family member by the hand and lead him/her over to the other family member, whereupon they are apt to hug one another. So many of the problems that arise in dysfunctional families center around just this kind of inability to demonstrate emotions to the others. This results in patients being constricted themselves and unable to give to their own families the kind of emotional demonstrativeness that is so sorely needed.

It is usually up to the therapist to determine when a family meeting has gotten too heavy or the participants are getting too tired. Occasionally, the participants themselves will say that they are getting tired or that too much is going on. In such case, the therapist should quickly conclude the meeting, but reiterating the problems that are then under discussion and making it clear that these will be picked up and continued in the next session.

Avoidance of Probable Conflict

I would recommend that one analyze the family situation very carefully before deciding which persons one will see together. One may have information that there are destructive combinations that repetitiously occur when a family gets together. If the patient is the one who is put down, the therapist can support him. If there is scapegoating going on between the parents, or if there is a parent who is emotionally explosive, it is better to first see the parents separately. It is then possible to foresee what attitudes and action might be encountered. The preliminary interviews can lay adequate groundwork so that one can proceed with confidence.

It is essential when considering joint sessions to have some idea whether the parents have other resources, in the way of relatives or personal friends that they might draw upon. Those parents who have been fighting for some years, and who have so discouraged their friends and relatives that they have become quite isolated, are a poor risk. They may now only have each other as the persons on whom they can depend. In such case, they may sometimes gang up on their adult child and defend one another, rather than being able to face the complaints and comments of the patient. This is a matter of sheer survival and it is understandable that they might do so. The therapist, however, should at all costs avoid such a situation because the outcomes can be negative for all concerned. It is probably better to choose the parent who seems to be the most approachable and see what can be done with that person.

The mother in one family was creating considerable difficulties in the present-day family of the patient because of

Hazardous Situations

her rigid views. Since she was felt to be fairly unpredictable and was apt to become highly emotional, the therapist decided to see her alone first.

Interview

THERAPIST: Mrs. Y., I am deeply appreciative of your coming all these hundreds of miles in order to talk with me and Richard. I decided to ask you to come in first and talk with me because I understand that there is a great deal of tension between you and Richard, partly over your religious attitudes, which Richard does not totally share, and also because I thought you might want to know something of what your son's situation is at this time.

MOTHER: Actually, I am very glad you asked me to come in alone, because I wanted to ask you a number of questions. I am awfully worried about Richard. He seems so depressed and so pale and haggard. How long has he been feeling this way?

THERAPIST: I would say that he has been depressed maybe for the last year and a half, but has only been acutely so in the last four months. I have been talking with him for the last month, and I felt that there were a number of things in his background that were unclear to me, and needed your help in tracking down really what had gone on. For one thing, I get the impression that most of the arguments and the general communication are between you and Richard, and that his father does not enter into it very much.

MOTHER: That's right. He is Mr. Smooth It All Over. He just backs out of every discussion and acts as though he wasn't even there. Although many times my husband is in disagreement with Richard, he would never know it. I speak up. Then when my husband gets me alone, he says I shouldn't have said that, I should have said that, and so we get into big arguments.

THERAPIST: I think we will probably have to find some way of resolving the differences between you and Richard about religious views. Would you be willing to talk with him about that?

MOTHER: Surely, I will. Anyway, to tell you the truth, I have turned to religion because my husband is so occupied in his business that he has not paid any attention to me or to the family for many years. He was willing to come on this trip because he is taking over 51 percent of a company here. I really would be glad to talk less about religion if only Richard and I could get along better. I really am anxious to meet with him, and I am grateful for the chance to talk with you a little about this first.

THERAPIST: I see that you have had some marital problems of your own. What stance do you think your husband will take in our joint session?

MOTHER: He will criticize me, as usual, and be very agreeable and very nice to Richard. He never takes any stand directly to Richard. He generally just tries to smooth everything over. He is considered very charming and very agreeable by other people—he is a real salesman. With me, however, he is critical and finds that almost everything I do is wrong. There is the possibility that in the meeting he is going to side with Richard against me. That's something I don't look forward to.

THERAPIST: I think maybe the best thing to do would be to talk to your husband alone before the joint sessions. If he has ideas of his own which he is not expressing, I would like to find them out before the meetings, so that we can encourage him to speak up.

DISCUSSION

The cooperation of the mother has been obtained in advance, and there are indications that she might have felt threatened if she had not had an opportunity to express her views in private. In view of her marital difficulties, she would have been very defensive, feeling that her husband was going to undercut her and side with the son against her. The mother went on to describe a good deal of what had gone on in the early family life of the patient. It appeared that the father was totally occupied building a business empire and that she had been forced to raise him practically by herself. The father had come from a highly critical family, and he found most of her child-rearing practices to be against his wishes. Because of that background, he refused to criticize Richard and confined himself to criticizing the mother's efforts.

The father was seen alone before the joint sessions because it was deemed important that mother and father felt that they had ample opportunity to state their views in privacy. The father appeared to feel that family management was entirely up to the mother. He tended to complain about what his wife and child did, but found it hard to focus on what opinion or action he would take. He was sincerely disturbed at the friction between his son and the mother, but evidently at no time had he attempted to assist in the resolution of the difficulty. It was agreed with both parents that the material they had given the therapist would be mentioned in the joint sessions.

As a result of these preliminary interviews, the joint sessions went smoothly, without friction between the parents, and the therapist could move back and forth freely between the information and background supplied by mother, father, and adult patient.

I am including here a part of Regina's letter that expresses her view of the separate parental interviews versus the joint parental–child interview.

Once we got to your office I felt much better and I am sure that they [parents] felt much worse. At least I was in somewhat familiar territory. I'm glad that we decided beforehand to talk to each parent individually first and then talk together. Talking to my father was good. I felt that he heard me and I really started to feel hopeful about getting things cleared up. We talked with him for over an hour. The combination of being so tired and starting to feel relieved that this wasn't going to all turn into something terrible made me feel really drained all of a sudden. In talking with my father, I was able to stay right there with him most of the time and not be intimidated when he would come back with something. When it was time to talk to my mother, I was getting tired and I know that I wasn't able to express myself as well to her as I had to my father.

When the three of us were together, I felt that they were very anxious to protect each other from any attacks [emphasis added]. I also felt it was more their time for challenging me with things that they were not satisfied with in me.

Right now the feelings are not as intense as they were then. I still do feel though that my father can hear me and help out. I know that for myself I feel much less frightened of them. I don't want to hurt them consciously, but I'm not going to build my lifestyle in a way that will completely suit them just to have their approval. I don't tell them everything that goes on in my life, but I'm not afraid to share some of me with them. I'm not getting on the next plane to move back home, but likewise I'm not packing to move to someplace more distant to get further away from them either.

9

Discussion of Sexual Problems with Older Parents

Sexual problems can be discussed with older parents after the adult child has gained enough confidence to explain clearly his or her own difficulties to the parent. There should be the development of open communication and desire to be mutually helpful as the underlying theme of the joint interview. It can be very risky if some concealed information comes to light that either party feels to be damaging to his/her personal image or to the relationship.

Case Example

Ramona was a married woman in her late twenties. The first few years of her marriage went very well, but in the last two years she had begun to feel negative about sexual relations with her husband. She had become depressed to a considerable degree and had been thinking lately that it would be best to obtain a divorce. She and her husband were seen conjointly. There appeared to be several contributing factors on his part and on Ramona's. He was initially very attentive and flattering in courtship and through the first few years of the marriage. Slowly, he began to revert to his family's pattern, which was to behave in a rather matter-of-fact way about the marital relationship. Affectionate gestures were restricted to perfunctory good-bye and good-night kisses. He was very involved in his work and tended to talk shop at home. His acquaintances were those who were co-workers in the engineering department, and when he invited them to the home, the conversation was unintelligible to Ramona since the shoptalk was highly technical. He had also become interested in some local political organizations, which required attending many night and Saturday meetings. Ramona became very resentful of these activities and inattention, withdrew emotionally, and became disinterested in sex. According to her husband, she had never been an active participant in sex and had seemed rather uncomfortable about it.

Ramona recounted in therapy some past experiences that were pertinent to her sexual attitudes. A year after she had left home to work and live in an apartment by herself, she had met Randy. He seemed to be a pleasant and agreeable person. They spent enjoyable times together dancing, etc., and it looked as though the dating would develop into a permanent relationship, marriage. It was on this understanding that Ramona had sexual relationships with Randy. Then she missed several menstrual periods. A number of unpleasant scenes followed as Ramona tried to talk to Randy about her anxiety and to discuss what to do. Randy became angry and accusative, implying that he was not responsible—someone else was. Ramona was crushed that he could think this, since she was a rather inhibited girl and had high moral standards. Randy told her to stop talking about it, he was not interested in getting married.

Ramona was worried sick. She was very reluctant to tell her mother about it, but she had no one else that she felt she could ask for help except mother. One of her reasons for hesitating in talking to her mother was a lifelong feeling that she had been a very heavy burden on her parents, that in some way her birth had very nearly ruined their lives.

She had had a series of illnesses up to the age of eight, and she remembered many arguments between her parents over the cost of her medical care. Perhaps this is why her father always had seemed to work so hard. He left early in the morning, returned for dinner, and then went back to the office. Certainly the family did not have a big house or really good furniture. Maybe it was Ramona's fault.

Mother was not a person who liked to talk about feelings. Ramona described her mother as a person who was busy at practical tasks all the time and whose attitudes were seldom evident about anything. When Ramona did talk to her mother finally, the experience was very upsetting. Mother became angry, accused Ramona of "'running around," didn't she know any better, what a shame to the family, etc. There was a scene with tears and mutual recriminations. Time proved, however, that Ramona was not pregnant after all. Relieved, she then broke off the relationship with Randy. His response was very traumatic to her. He said she was a failure as a sex partner anyway. She had no feminine traits, wasn't pretty or a good dancer or conversationalist, and much more.

The result of this experience was distrust in men and a suspicion that a man's interest was only in sex. She concluded that her mother thought her to be gullible and her morals questionable. Ramona felt used by men and that her worth was doubtful since her mother had reacted so critically about the situation. They now had an uneasy, tentative relationship. However, Ramona wanted to ask her mother about her attitudes toward sex and so asked that she join us in a joint interview. When mother came she seemed nervous and anxious.

Interview

THERAPIST: Ramona, have you told your mother about your difficulties in your marriage? I want to be sure she understands what we are concerned with.

RAMONA: Yes, I did. I am not interested in sex, mother, and that is causing friction between Doug and myself. I have been thinking a lot lately about the time when I was going around with Randy. I think it has affected my attitude towards men. Then another thing I thought about was the fighting between you and dad when I was little. It was about money, and it had something to do with the doctor bills for me. I've always felt rather guilty for being born.

MOTHER: But those quarrels weren't about you.

RAMONA: But I remember hearing them. There wasn't enough money somehow. What was it about, if it wasn't about me?

MOTHER: It was about your father's first wife and their children. She kept asking for more and more money and he kept agreeing to it so it really put us into difficulties with all the bills we had. Your father wasn't making much money at that time. He's always worked too hard as it is, and the pressure on him to earn more has been extreme. He told me that his first marriage was a forced one because of her pregnancy. She's been a problem through the years.

RAMONA: You mean you were mad at him for sending her money?

MOTHER: Yes, I think he was too easy a touch and gave her much more than she was entitled to by the divorce decree. He should have stood up to her.

RAMONA: But dad doesn't like unpleasantness or disagreements. That's why I only talked to you about Randy. You really hurt my feelings when you were so critical.

MOTHER: Well, it really upset me. It brought back all those unpleasant times in past years. Besides, it didn't need to happen. Randy wasn't much good. I don't know what you saw in him.

RAMONA: I don't either now, but it made me feel as though sex wasn't really a good thing.

MOTHER: I didn't know how to deal with that whole mess.

RAMONA: You've never mentioned sex to me. Do you feel it's OK and a good thing?

MOTHER: Well, it's a part of nature, I guess. It seems to me it isn't all that important in life and your father and I have had our problems that way. He doesn't like to talk about such things, you know. I suppose sex is a normal part of life when you're married, but I think people put too much importance on it.

THERAPIST: And when you were first married, the subject of sex and marital relationship caused you a lot of pain because of your husband's first child and his first wife.

MOTHER: Yes, and it seems to me he should have been more loyal to me and Ramona. All his working has just left us alone.

Discussion

Ramona first approached her relationship with her mother—had she been resented all these years as a financial burden? When that was cleared up she inquired about mother's attitudes toward sex. As mother explained, she saw mother feel that in marriage there is apt to be sex without a good personal relationship. This made Ramona think of her own marriage, which seemed to be developing in the same direction. She felt stronger after this meeting with her mother, and less guilty for being alive when she knew the family background. There were more joint sessions with her husband, who altered his behavior so that Ramona felt she was being treated as a person, not just a sex object. From this point on, her sexual functioning greatly improved. Ramona's mother changed her attitudes toward her daughter to a very considerable degree. She became gentler, more supportive, and was open about discussing sexual matters with Ramona. Their contacts became mutually satisfying.

Incest

Incest is one of the most difficult situations met in a therapist's practice. Social taboos about incest make it difficult for patients to reveal such a history and generally preclude any satisfactory resolution or relationships between those who were involved in such a problem. The participants in incestuous relationships are usually a stepfather, father, brother, or grandfather and a young girl. Usually also, the situation could best be described as rape-incest. Occasionally, I have also known male patients whose fathers have made homosexual incestuous advances toward them, but I have not had the experience of directly discussing such an occurrence with the parent and child, as I have had with female patients.

I encountered victims of incestuous relationships when I worked in the state mental hospitals, and found those women to have been severely damaged psychologically. At that time I felt the damage to be irreparable. Since those days, I have changed my opinions by virtue of my experience in talking jointly with parent and child about incestuous incidents.

An incestuous advance delivers a smashing, destructive blow to the self-esteem and identity of the recipient. A child or an adult presumes and expects that his birthright is the care and protection of his parents and blood relatives. In the vast majority of lives, this expectation is fulfilled. In those where it is not, the individual feels cheated, demeaned, unloved, and discounted as a worthwhile person. Some of those women who submit to incestuous advances participate out of fear. Some participate with the dim hope that a small measure of approval or esteem can be obtained from the parent or blood relative. Obviously, incest does not occur in a normally functioning family with open communication, respect for individuality, and mutual caring. Small morsels of approval can therefore seem to be of value to a patient in dysfunctional families even though obtained at such a high cost.

The scarcity of affection and esteem in a dysfunctional family inhibits a cry for help. Girls are afraid to appeal to their mothers for help if a sexual advance has been made by a father, brother, or grandfather because they fear to be disbelieved or to be blamed for what has happened. Incidentally, in my experience, there has been a substantial number of grandfathers who have sexually molested their young granddaughters. The respect for, and presumed probity of, older persons additionally inhibits the granddaughter from speaking to her mother and asking for help. Years later, the story is revealed to the girl's physician or to a psychotherapist. If the latter, something can be done about it.

Mothers are in a difficult position when there are incestuous relationships between the child and her husband or a male blood relative. The mother's own self-esteem as wife and mother is attacked. What if the child has made a false accusation? What recourse does the wife and mother have if she ascertains the child's statement to be true? She may not have the psychological, financial, and social resources to do anything about the situation. If she feels so, the course she may choose is to not hear or not comprehend what the child tells her or what she may deduce for herself. If a mother does not take cognizance or action on behalf of her child, the consequences to the child are extremely severe. It is a final refutation of the child's worth, a message that mother doesn't love or care about him, or that the child's perception of reality is distorted and valueless.

I should like to give you a case example that will demonstrate that such an incestuous situation can be talked about directly and that the results can be highly constructive. In this woman's case, and I shall call her Electra, the daughter, mother, and stepfather have all gained in self-esteem, communication, confrontation skills, and assurance that the other person cares about him or her.

Case Example

Electra came to me because she was very depressed. Her relationships with others were tentative, and she generally found herself making all of the adjustments to please someone. At bottom, she felt her judgment to be questionable, her opinions not worthwhile, and it seemed to her that no one really thought much about her or particularly cared about her. She was socially inactive and felt afraid of men.

Electra's history explained why she felt this way about herself. She lost her own father through divorce when she was five and gained a stepfather at age eight. Her mother seemed very much in love with her stepfather. In discussing child–parent relationships, the mother had said early in Electra's life that she would choose her husband over her children because the children would leave and it was to mother's advantage to remain with the husband, who would be with her longer. When Electra reached teen-age years, her stepfather made sexual advances to her. She was quite frightened and desperate to do something about it because her mother worked, and during those times when her mother was gone, the stepfather approached her. She tried to explain it to her mother, but I suspect that she talked in such a roundabout manner that the mother did not fully understand it. At any rate, nothing was done about it and Electra spent much time avoiding her stepfather. She began to be doubtful of her mother's love for her and the situation was sufficiently tense that she moved away from home. Significantly, the stepfather was displeased and said that it indicated that something was wrong at home. One presumes that he was feeling guilty. Electra then moved many states away and established herself with one blood relative contact that was very beneficial to her.

Although I have treated other women who have suffered from incestuous experiences, I have chosen Electra's case because I am able to have it described to you in Electra's own words. In addition, she is a person who expresses herself very well and her letter describes very vividly the process of meeting with the mother and its favorable outcome. I may say also that I have the utmost admiration for her mother, whom I consider to be a woman of extraordinary courage and deep love for her daughter, and a sincere and honest person.

When I sat down to put my experience into words, I found it very difficult to transfer my feelings from my head and heart onto the paper. I am certain that once I have completed this I will think of so many things I have forgotten.

At the time the idea of a confrontation with my mother was suggested to me, my mind spun into circles and I said an adamant NO. *My emotions ran the gamut from great confusion and fear to one of exciting yet painful anticipation.*

One of the strongest fears was—could I tell her of the bizarre things my stepfather had done after keeping it bottled inside of me for so many years. I loved my mother very much and did not want to hurt her, but I knew that it would, very deeply. Another fear was—would she believe me? She had always told me that in a marriage the husband should come first, as the marriage vows stated, "to forsake all others." Therefore, if there had to be a choice between husband and children, the husband would have to be first. Would she forsake me if I told her? Would she hate me for even suggesting that such a thing happened at all? Would she accept it?

I had tried to tell her before in my teenage, clumsy, subtle way, but she interpreted it as something other than what I meant, with an explanation that satisfied only her.

The most confused and thought provoking fear which was important to me was the problems, or even divorce, I could cause in their marriage. I loved them both very much and though my stepfather had done this thing, I tried very hard to separate this part of him from the loving and understanding man who had reared me from the age of seven and treated me as though I were his own. I did not want to lose another father through divorce as I did my real father.

The painful anticipation was the telephone call to my mother asking her to fly out here. To my surprise she said, "yes," without too many questions.

My mother arrived and the next day we went to the interview. I was extremely nervous and filled with anxiety. Lee asked me to tell mother what my stepfather had done because then she would understand why I was so upset and why I needed her so. The words stuck in my throat. They just wouldn't come out. Lee saw that I was in a hopeless position and explained to my mother that my stepfather had made sexual advances to me. The result of it was that I wasn't sure of my self worth and I couldn't relate to men. For years I wondered why did he do this to me? At the same time, I wondered whether she would believe me and if she would think it was my fault. Her first reaction was shocked silence. The second reaction was that she said immediately that she did believe me. I cried with relief. I repeated what she had told me as a child about husbands coming first. She immediately responded by saying that I had misinterpreted that statement and I did come first. She would even divorce him if necessary. I was absolutely stunned and taken aback. It was so different from what I had expected. From thereon we interchanged feelings.

I explained to her how distraught I had been all these years. It was 65% of the reason why I left home. I repeatedly told her that I loved her and I did not want to hurt her. Most of all I did not want her to get a divorce. She told me that she loved me, but that she wanted to talk to him as soon as she returned home. She felt it was her responsibility to handle it. The emotional impact of our discussion was tremendous. We cried together, a loving, sharing cry.

She then asked me who else knew about the experience. I told her that my aunt and uncle knew and the group members.[1] She went directly to my aunt and uncle and discussed it. She began to feel better. On her own she asked to come to the next group meeting with me.

At the group meeting, she repeated that she supported me and loved me. In return the group supported her. She again asked me why I hadn't told her before. I explained that I did try. She admitted that it was possible that she hadn't understood. With the group's help, we realized that years ago neither one of us could have coped with it.

My mother left to return home one week later. My stepfather picked her up at the airport. Before they had reached their home, she told him she knew what he had done. I received another surprise. He admitted it! He said he had felt guilty about it and was extremely sorry that it had happened. He said that he did not understand why he did it. He felt that perhaps it was my strong resemblance to my mother. He was really sorry that he had hurt me.

They proceeded together to work on the problem from that point on. I feel from appearances and from what I have heard from my mother, that their

---

[1] Electra belonged to one of my group therapy units.

relationship is deeper now than before. My relationship with them has grown over the last few years into one of honesty, freedom, and openness.

In restrospect as the years go on, I feel the benefits of this experience practically every day. I am now less inhibited with men. I am not afraid to speak up. I like myself much more now and I say a lot more positive things about myself.

Finally me,
Electra

I feel that the experience of Electra, her mother, and her stepfather is a constructive experience from a multitude of viewpoints. The outstanding quality of all three persons was their honesty, courage, and willingness to do something about a situation that pained all of them. I suggest it as one model for the solution of similar problems of incest.

Homosexuality

Concerning homosexuality, I have met conjointly with my patient and his parent, when the parent has had a fair idea that his adult child has been a practising homosexual. The meetings have focused not on the homosexual behavior but rather on the frictions between adult child and parent. This has seemed to me to be the important part of the meeting, for the relationship of parent and child determines identity, self-worth, and often definition of oneself as male or female. Sexual identity and behavior is taught early in childhood by such external means as clothing and hair dress. Those parents who encourage female dress for boys confuse the child not only about his sexual identity but also about how to relate to the parent. Sexuality is learned most significantly by parental definitions of male/female roles, such as dominance and submission, self-assertion, or self-punishment. Sometimes the root of homosexual leanings is based upon the child's experience that the parent of the opposite sex is emotionally inaccessible to him. Consequently, the most desirable goal of conjoint meetings is to achieve improvements in parent–child relationships that will enhance the patient's self-esteem.

The patient also achieves a better perspective on those early childhood experiences that influence his sexual life. New information and changes in self-perception then may determine whether he wishes to change his sexual orientation. Some of my patients have become heterosexual; some have remained homosexual.

The meetings about which I speak have been with homosexual patients who were aware of relationship problems in their past and present lives. Such patients were actively seeking to improve their emotional well-being and their relationships with others. In my experience, those homosexuals who were involved in "cruising" or sadomasochistic practices were less attuned to working out their emotional relationships than they were to acting out maneuvers, or to manipulations of their various homosexual contacts. They may have sought individual therapy, sometimes group therapy, but not conjoint meetings with family members. I therefore have not had experience with such persons in adult child–parent meetings. Among other barriers to this kind of meeting, I find that aggressive homosexuals are usually without many personal resources—close friends, relatives, or personal satisfactions through jobs, interests, etc. It is understandable that conjoint family meetings are far too threatening for them to contemplate.

I report my experience to date. It may be that I will have such meetings with parent and adult child in the future.

10

Two Additional Uses of the Method

Emotional Separation and Divorce Crises

Psychotherapists, expecially those who engage in marital counseling, often find themselves in the position of trying to cope with the emotional crises of a newly separated or newly divorced patient. Such patients are often desperately lonely to the point of suicidal thoughts. Their emotional lifelines have been cut, resulting in a severe state of shock. The necessity of making new and different living arrangements, of presenting oneself as single in social situations, and the loss of accustomed familial support systems contribute to feelings of acute disorientation. The very sense of identity is often severely shaken.

Loss of social identity is more generally true of women than of men, given our cultural system, which defines nonworking wives by the place of their activity—namely, housewives. Being a wife has social status, mostly gained through the alliance to the husband and his occupation. The wife's social status rises and falls in consonance with the occupational status of her husband, and not necessarily only in the financial sense. A nonworking wife can therefore be suddenly bereft of social identity should her husband leave her, or if she leaves of her own volition. I have frequently heard the fear and anguish in the voice of the middle-aged woman as she says, "Who would want an older woman like me, untrained in anything? Who would hire me for any job at all?"

She is partly right, for it is not easy for such a woman to find work or even training for work, in spite of increasing governmental and volunteer community programs that offer vocational training. Younger women are initially frightened and as lost as the older women. They tend to recover more rapidly, however. It is my observation that they try to reestablish as quickly as possible their social status via shifting alliances with men. Possibly they hope to reestablish themselves in their accustomed role of wife and housewife. Unfortunately, it is generally true that these quick alliances do not prove out for more than a few weeks or months.

The men who suffer so acutely in the separation or divorce crises are those who are overly dependent upon their wives. Usually the excessive dependency lies in the emotional realm. Such men see their wives as mother figures, or they may have such restricted emotional lives themselves that they live vicariously through their wives. The experienced therapist thinks immediately of certain occupational groups—engineers, scientists, computer programmers and technicians, surgeons, and accountants. The "Lockheed syndrome" is familiar to those who practice in any area containing a large number of professional engineers. An essential element of the Lockheed syndrome is an emotionally restricted engineer married to a woman who is often somewhat overemotional, self-deprecating, and self-punishing. A breakup in such marriages usually produces an acutely depressed, clingingly dependent, emotionally disoriented man.

It is interesting that this desperate situation occurs in spite of my warnings that separation will produce loneliness, disorientation, etc. Perhaps it is due to the fantasy of personal invulnerability that we all seem to have. Other men who participate in a military offensive may be killed, but certainly not *me*. Highway accidents only happen to other people. Smoking kills other people, not *me*. Most probably, however, the explanation lies in the fact there is no way to really know how separation feels, except to feel it.

The most acutely depressed persons are naturally those who did not make close personal friends and did not reveal their inner feelings to others. They may have many acquaintances at work, but now they shrink from saying, "I'm divorced, I'm separated, I'm lonely." Overly dependent persons naturally do not have many close confidants or they would not be overly dependent. They would have developed security points in their lives had they not been restricted personalities. One therefore finds such persons come to a crisis where all of the eggs are in one basket and the basket has dropped.

There are several alternatives and recourses available to the patient and the therapist. Antidepressant medication is invaluable. There are also those patients who tend to go it alone and will watch TV endlessly. Others try bar-hopping and excessive drinking. Transient romances and sexual affairs blossom and die in rapid succession. Therapists often refer the patient to some helpful organization, such as Parents Without Partners, or to professional therapy groups designed to offer discussion and support to separated and divorced individuals. The patient's acute hunger for closeness is seldom satisfied by any of these resources.

I have increasingly used a method of fostering closeness between my patient and one of his or her siblings. Ordinarily, the acutely lonely person does not have a close, warm relationship with his parents, and usually not with his sisters and brothers. In his fragile state, the patient often is very reluctant to encounter his parents or to ask them for aid and emotional support. When I suggest that we talk to a brother or sister to open an avenue of communication and emotional sharing, the patient seems intrigued and hopeful. He is often aware that his sibling is suffering from the same lack of closeness, and that the sibling has had personal tragedies of his or her own.

To the patient, as well as to me, it seems logical to start working on the development of emotional exchanges between siblings. Patients are often much more willing for such a joint interview to take place with their siblings than they are to encounter their parents. Following discussions, siblings may spend much time together companionably. During those times, they recall both good and bad times they shared in their childhood families and their marriages. Many submerged feelings surface to be jointly explored, feelings about their parents, feelings about themselves, feelings about each other. The result of these interchanges is a closer, warmer, more open, more understanding relationship. Both are giving to the other something that they lacked in their childhood family experience.

It is precisely this aspect of the interchange between siblings that is most important. The person who is terrified and lonely as the result of a separation might have someone to talk to (often not), but such a relationship can often be described as one-way. That is, the frightened, needy, separated person is asking for help, asking for emotional support to be given to *him*. The other person is getting little in return, although he may feel glad that he is able to help a friend. Brothers and sisters, however, are giving to one another because they already have a bond between them and have usually wanted to make that bond more confident, satisfying, and mutually enjoyable.

Such newly developing sibling relationships are of great help to the woman who feels socially alienated. She is more able, on such improvement, to take action on her own behalf in both practical and psychological areas. The isolated man obtains the same beneficial results. As he feels that he has some continuing contacts with a sibling, that he is not alone in the world, he begins to feel he can reach out for more friends and acquaintances. He reenters the social

stream of life feeling less like a failure or a rejected person.
Some illustrations from cases of mine may make this clearer.

Case Example

Tina had had an unsuccessful marriage for some years. She had been married at rather a young age and had really married to please her family. The husband was a very successful businessman but lacked the qualities that contribute to a successful marriage. He was unable to compliment Tina and instead criticized her most of the time. He was nondemonstrative to her and the children, rather finicky about what pleased him, and peremptory in his demands. Tina was self-depreciatory because of her childhood experiences, so she accepted many of the criticisms as undoubtedly true. Her own parents had constantly criticized her and she had felt disliked and as though she were a quite unacceptable person. Consequently, it was unthinkable to her that she should question her parents' views of her, or that she should express her own opinions or make known her own wants. From her childhood training, these attitudes about herself were continued in her relationships with other persons, as well as with her husband.

In spite of such thorough training, the unthinkable happened. Tina was so utterly depressed and miserable in her marriage that she began to question what was going on. Was she really that worthless? Once her questioning had started, and with two brief contacts separated by a year's time with me, Tina proceeded to the point of separation and filing for divorce. Then she came to see me again and I was faced with an extremely lonely and isolated woman. She was severed from all of her husband's social contacts and emotionally unsupported by her parents. Fortunately, there were some friends who could be developed into close, supportive allies. Tina's identity was shaky, however, and she felt alienated from her family.

I suggested we meet with the sister with whom she was closest. She usually kept in contact with the sister by telephone, and sister was coming to visit. The meeting was very productive. Tina's perception of her family was verified. Sister said specifically that from her earliest memories she had recognized that Tina had been picked on and bullied by her mother and father. Neither sister knew why. All the other children had ended up with severe psychological problems, so one would assume that things were not well with the parents' marriage. Tina's sister, whom I shall call Theresa, had received her share of criticism. It was very sad for me to see that Theresa had developed even more psychological handicaps than had Tina. In spite of a successful career, Theresa had even fewer emotional contacts than her sister. The meeting gave both sisters an opportunity to move closer to one another emotionally, in spite of their respective difficulties. They continue their closer relationship, and feelings on both sides are more open and freely available to the other. Tina's life has improved greatly in many areas. She is happier, more active socially, more self-assured and self-reliant. Here is Tina's report:

Dear Dr. Headley
When the idea of having members of my family in to see you was first brought up, my feelings about it were mixed. I thought it would be very good as far as letting you see for yourself the way my family sees me and how they relate in general. It is difficult to describe the complexities and atmosphere of a family situation and I was glad you would have an opportunity to see some things for yourself. On the other hand, I was apprehensive. If I had been more aware of her present state of mind I am not sure how I would have reacted.
As for the meeting itself, while it was painful for me and for my sister, I feel it was a very positive experience. Mostly because it was the first time I was sure it wasn't just my imagination. And only someone in my family, who saw things firsthand could confirm that what I felt had been going on, was true. It also took away a lot of the guilt I had felt over having critical opinions of my parents and family situation. It helped remove many doubts.
I also gained an entirely new insight into my sister. I knew she had a great

deal of pain—I just never realized how much. It also helped me to be able to understand the strain our relationship seemed to come under during her visit. Yet I also know we'll get past it, and I think and hope we'll be even closer. We just both have much to sort out of our individual selves. I think if we do that the relationship will find itself.

I'm sure I gained a great deal more from it than I am able to articulate here. It's amazing to me, but I am no longer afraid of meeting with my parents. I'm not sure how much they'll be able to give (or take). I still love them (and I'll try to give this to them), but there won't be any more strings. I'm not a puppet anymore. I'm real.

Tina

Manuel's wife came to see me about her imminent decision to divorce Manuel. She described him as totally intellectual, a person who must weigh everything logically. If her feelings did not seem logical to him, they were dismissed as either nonexistent or as unworthy of consideration. She felt she was living with a "reasoning machine." While divorce was frightening for her to contemplate, it seemed a more desirable alternative than continuing life in this style. She expressed her opinions to Manuel directly in our joint marital meetings. He barely "heard" her and found it incredible and illogical that she might leave him. He did, however, accept enough of what she told him so that he started working with me to see what could be done about his unemotional and mechanistic way of behaving. Every step of the way was hard for Manuel. His childhood family had trained him to block out everything except the reasoning process and in particular to block out anything that sounded negative. In spite of some progress, I heard from the wife that she could not stand much more. Despite Manuel's sincere effort, for which she gave him full credit, she felt the whole process was too slow and too late.

Manuel became more and more panic-stricken as he saw the separation coming. He could not turn to his parents. They had already ignored his first intimations that the marriage was breaking up. He felt he could not expect any support from that quarter. He had acquaintances and one person who could qualify as a friend, but that person was also a co-worker, which presented difficulties.

I suggested to Manuel that we talk with his sister, who lives an hour's drive away from him. Sister had experienced a divorce herself and in addition we knew that she had some of the same problems in expressing her emotions as did Manuel. I felt such a meeting would be very helpful to the sister, as well as to Manuel. Manuel was doubtful, questioning the whole idea. He decided to try it and it worked out very well. I quote from Manuel's letter;

> I was both surprised and mildly apprehensive when the proposal was first made to have a joint session with my sister. I did not know what to expect. It was difficult for me to work up the courage to call her and to reveal that we were having marital problems. I was not at all sure that she would be willing to participate in a joint session. However, I desperately needed someone with whom I could be close and I looked forward to the possibility of developing a closer relationship with my sister.
>
> During the interview, I felt somewhat ill at ease. I felt sorry for my sister because she was in a strange environment and Dr. Headley tended to press her for certain [feeling] responses. I felt considerable pain when my sister said that she thought I was a cold person. It really felt good to be able to release the warm feelings that I had for my sister and to reveal my desires for a closer relationship.
>
> The joint session was very productive in that the interchange brought out facts and opinions about the family, how they interacted with each other, and how these interactions may have affected our behaviors. It seemed that my sister had a clearer view of our parents than I did, and had years ago rejected them (especially mother) as a model for her. Although I could not remember his behaving that way, my sister's description of how father interacted with her when there were differences of opinion was perfectly similar to how I interacted with my wife. The joint session revealed that my sister and I had common personality defects. Since the joint session, my sister and I have maintained frequent contact. Already the relationship is much closer than it ever was, and it is continuing to develop. I have found that she is a good, sympathetic listener and I have been able to unburden marital problems with her. More and more we are able to discuss and reveal feelings. Sometimes my sister seems quite reserved and it takes a little while to warm up the situation. Hopefully, we will be able to provide each other emotional support, to help each other with our common problems and to assist each other in dealing with our parents.
>
> *Manuel*

Here then, is another example of the value inherent in returning to the source of one's difficulties. Childhood families can be destructive in their effect. Given the chance, they can also be eminently constructive in a most unique and irreplacable way.

I have a letter from Manuel's sister describing the experience from her point of view.

> *In reconstructing our joint brother–sister session, I am certainly impressed by the changes that have occurred in our relationship in the short time since.*
>
> *When my brother first suggested the meeting, I was anxious to come and to help him in any way that I could. I did feel that having already uncovered some of the family problems in my own therapy, I might be able to confirm the ideas he was beginning to discover for himself. If I was disturbed about the prospect of the meeting, it was mostly as to his state of mind and his fear that I might not be willing to attend.*
>
> *At the beginning of the interview, I was a little ill at ease. However, as we progressed I felt increasingly at ease and could quickly see the benefits. It is a more direct type of therapy than I am accustomed to, and it took me a little time to adjust.*
>
> *There is no question that my brother and I feel closer now than we ever have. I certainly see him opening up in whole new areas. Obviously, he is working very hard at it, because he feels he has something precious to gain in his marriage. We are much more in touch than we have been and on a more meaningful level. I think we will continue to stay that way. When his current crisis is more under control, I am sure we will establish an even better two-way communication, to which I am looking forward.*
>
> *Letitia*

Manuel, feeling strengthened by his improved relationship with his sister, next met with his parents and myself. Contrary to his expectations, they have tried hard to alter their attitudes and behavior toward him, his sister, and his wife. Manuel made significant changes in his own personality functioning as a result of these new perceptions and experiences. Two months after the separation took place, his wife was sufficiently impressed by the changes that she felt she would like to work on the marriage with the "new" Manuel.

Present Intergenerational Family Frictions

Frictions between the nuclear family (adult child) and grandparents (older parents) are quite common, even though the two groups may not live in the same town or in fact may be separated by hundreds of miles. Their contacts may be via telephone, letters, gifts, or occasional visits. If one listens to the average group at such places as an employees' coffee room or a large social gathering, one frequently hears about the conflicts between parent and grandparents over raising of the grandchildren. Those syndicated columnists who publish letters from troubled persons deal fully as often with adult child–older parent dissatisfactions as they do with "lovelorn."

Anyone can easily think of typical situations of this sort. Some grandparents seem to forget that their children are grown up and enter their children's home without announcing themselves. They take over the kitchen and start rearranging things to suit themselves, give instructions on how to do everything, or try to monopolize their children's time. They are most apt to become involved in the disciplining of the grandchildren and to protest that the parents are either too lax or too strict. Frequently the problem lies in grandparents being too indulgent of the grandchildren, for now they look back at their own parenting experience and want to be very generous to their grandchildren both in gifts and in excusing misbehavior.

One should also recognize that adult children are also problems to grandparents. They may make unreasonable demands upon grandparents' time and financial resources or be thoughtless about their treasured belongings. Some adult children do not show respect for older parents' dignity and dismiss their views as unimportant or ridiculous, and may neglect their emotional and social needs. This discussion is intended to emphasize that whenever there is an unhappy relationship in a family group—adult child, older parent, relatives, in-laws, etc.—joint meetings with professional help may better the situation.

It has been the traditional practice in individual and marital couple therapy that therapists do not become directly involved in these two-family disagreements.* However, I suggest that it can be very helpful to do so, even if the parent of the adult child must come from several states away, and conjoint sessions can bring about solutions to annoying disagreements and change the basic relationships in a beneficial way. The therapist acts as a mediator, facilitator, friend, and often as an educator to all the persons involved. Usually the families are so enmeshed in their problems that they cannot get beyond their convictions to see any value in other family members' viewpoints. The addition of a professional person outside of the family circle creates a calmer, more objective atmosphere at the outset of any conjoint meetings and the therapist can keep discussion to the point as well as control excessive emotional exchanges. The focus of the interactions changes from whose ideas are going to prevail to how a mutually satisfactory agreement can be reached.

The methodology of such conjoint meetings is similar to those that have been described. The first problem is to get the two families or individuals in the family to consider such a meeting. On the part of the nuclear family (the adult child and/or spouse) several typical objections arise. First, of course, is a reluctance to get into a direct confrontation because it might be very upsetting to everyone and might leave many hurt feelings to jeopardize the family relationships. There is also a good deal of trepidation at undertaking such an untried method. Obviously, these families are not used to constructive confrontations and negotiations or their problem would not have arisen in the first

---

*Family therapy with children may include grandparents when they are living in the family, or nearby.

place. Some feel that it is almost like deserting their parent(s) or in-laws if a meeting is suggested, on the supposition that taking an independent viewpoint or position will seem like separation and alienation. Others fear that a confrontation will most likely result in all the ill feeling being directed at the spouse, who will be seen as the instigator of all the trouble.

It is essential that the nuclear family (adult child and spouse) have succinctly in mind what the objectional behavior is, so that communication is clear. Similarly, there should be alternate suggested behavior and means of effecting a mutual accommodation. If both spouses are to be at the conjoint meeting, they should agree to share equally in the discussion and have some agreed-upon understanding of what their opening approach to the older parent(s) will be. The nature of the problem will determine to some degree which groups of family members will be seen conjointly. In conflicts over the grandchildren, it is probably well to have both nuclear parents present; flexibility on this point should depend on the nature and history of the conflict and the personalities involved. The limits of negotiation should also be decided upon in advance. The adult child of the grandparent group should take responsibility for firm stands in the nuclear family and not leave it up to the spouse. The spouse would obviously be blamed by the grandparents if he or she issued the ultimatum.

Once there is a clear understanding of which problems to tackle, what the alternative solutions may be, how the family members are to be approached, and who is to be present, it is the responsibility of the concerned individual to contact the older parent (or other relative) and suggest the meeting.

When the individuals are present and the discussion opens, however, responsibility should shift largely to the therapist. He should be sure at the outset that the purpose of the meeting is clear, underscore its constructive intent, and keep discussion to the point. He will need to balance the forces within the family group, being sure not to let emotions get destructively out of hand. He must always be searching for ways whereby the participants can understand one another better, and find ways that will help them make adjustments to each other. He may often have to take a stand, such as to affirm that the nuclear family's first responsibility is spouse to spouse and to their young children. If so, he may need to help older parents relinquish their dependence on, and control of, the adult child. It usually is also advisable to lay the groundwork for future discussions if problems arise, as many "limping" families need support and assistance over further joint problems.

Struggles with grandparents over treatment of grandchildren has often been based on driving emotional needs of the grandparents. Some grandparents seem to have more emotional investment in the grandchildren than they do in their own children, whom they may take for granted. Favoritism, pursuit of an interest of the grandparents, and overindulgence are usually based on some unmet need in the grandparents. Conjoint meetings of nuclear family and grandparents can suggest redirection or modification of the grandparents' needs. Sometimes the emotional need is too great for modification. In such case, the adult child may have to take a forceful stand based on the children's needs and serve notice that the grandparents are not welcome to visit unless they pay heed to the nuclear parents' requests.

I recall, for example, a situation in which both grandparents favored the first child. They played with her, brought presents, and exclaimed at the child's abilities. The second daughter was all but ignored. The parents soon noticed that their second child withdrew into her room soon after the grandparents visited, and for the following two days seemed withdrawn and listless. Alarm on the parents' part soon changed to anger. In the discussion between nuclear parents and grandparents there was little rapprochement. The grandparents tended to deny what the parents saw happening. Finally, the son said to his parents that if it was necessary to choose between the happiness of his child and a relationship with his parents, he had to choose his child. This meant an ultimatum to the grandparents that they were not to visit as long as their behavior persisted.

It was a very tense three months between the two families. The grandparents, having the greatest need for the relationship, gradually moved toward reconciliation. There were some interim strategies, such as the grandparents being allowed to have only one child visiting at a time. The parents made sure to watch the grandparents' behavior closely and spoke up immediately if they saw any return of favoritism. It remained a somewhat difficult situation for quite a while but the needs of the two families achieved an uneasy balance. In this case the nuclear parents were closely allied and the son had sufficient courage to stand by his ultimatum. The presence of the therapist served as a support to the nuclear parents and tempered some of the resistance of the grandparents. It set a tone of negotiation for new relationships, rather than recriminations, and assisted in the subsequent management of the situation.

Summary

Many of these parent–grandparent or parent–relative problems could be successfully dealt with in conjoint sessions around specific issues, time-limited to one to three interviews, with a skillful therapist. The public might well be interested in such services if they were aware of the short-term nature of the contact. Many people avoid seeking professional help in such matters because they conceive of psychotherapeutic help as lengthy and analytical. Since many of the participants in these interfamilial frictions are getting along quite satisfactorily in their lives, they do not see a need for an intermediary. Usually nuclear parents are the ones who are worried and seek help for their problem, but both parties stand to gain from a professionally guided resolution of these conflicting needs. All too often, families settle the matter by ceasing contact or by moving out of town.

11

Procedures and Follow-Up with Patient and Parent

Arrangement for Meetings

When the therapist and patient have agreed that it is time to include the older parents, it is always my arrangement to have the patients get in touch with their relatives and ask them to come. Patient and therapist discuss the kind of material that might be brought out in the meeting and it is then up to the patient to say to his parents or siblings in advance which of this material is to be discussed. Generally, the patient will tell his parents that he is seeing a therapist and that there are some problems in his treatment that need some help from the parents, and would the parents come. Occasionally, where there is an ongoing problem between parent and child, the patient will say that the problems are getting acute and that he would like to work them out directly with the parent in the presence of the therapist. I do not believe that it would be helpful for the therapist to call the patient's parents or relatives and ask them to come. For one thing, it gives no gauge of the patient's willingness to speak to his relatives. Secondly, it would give the opportunity for the patient to back out at some crucial point and say that this meeting was not his idea but the therapist's.

Experience has been that in spite of all the negative prognostications of the patient, parents practically never refuse to come. As a matter of fact, in all the years of my use of this methodology, there has been only one mother who refused to come, although the father in that family did come.

There is a percentage of patients who can never work up the courage to face their parents or relatives. Some of these go through long delaying tactics and state that they have made some entrée into asking their parents to come for joint sessions, but evidently this was not a clear message, nor was it a strong message, because the matter drags on and on. The therapist may ask frequently whether the parents are intending to come and the patient will put it off. Another large group of patients think the idea over and go through a cycle of first negation, then interest, then a weighing back and forth whether it would be a good idea, and then a procrastination. Many of these people, when pressed to decide whether they wish to meet after it has been discussed for some time, decide that for many reasons they do not wish to venture such an approach. An oft-repeated reason is "I don't really want my mother or my father to know that I'm having this much psychiatric problem. They are against psychiatry anyway, and it's going to put me in bad if they know that I am seeking help." Actually, many of these parents have a pretty good idea that the patient has sought psychiatric help, so this is obviously not a true reason. More often, the patients like to keep secret from their parents many of their activities and thoughts, and open communication would endanger their small island of safety.

Another group of people really do not like to work agressively on their own behalf. They are much more inclined to talk about their difficulties, to complain, and to make small steps of improvement than they are to take a large, aggressive step such as this. They may be persons who are not very vital in their general life-style and who can only proceed in a small one-step-at-a-time manner. Most of them are fairly allergic to change and do not really want to alter their life-style in any major way. Family confrontations, they feel, might put such an obligation upon them and so they do not really pursue requesting that parents and relatives come to join them.

Patients have the inalienable right to refuse this method of treatment if they feel sufficiently opposed to it. It is analogous to the situation of the patient who is contemplating separation and divorce. I never urge a definite action upon such a patient, but emphasize that he must make up his own mind because he is the one who will bear the consequences. Patients are intimately aware of their own abilities and their limits of tolerance for emotional stress. All of us do not have equal abilities and tolerances. While I might feel that such a meeting would be advantageous to my patient, I honor their right to self-determination. And who can tell? In the absence of direct incontrovertible information, perhaps their evaluations of themselves and their parents is the correct one. I am not, therefore, saying that those who refuse the confrontation with their parents are sicker than those who agree.

Americans are noted for their mobile population shifts. People are constantly moving from one home locality to another to relocate themselves for new job assignments, educational training, retirement, or health reasons. Frequently, older parents may reside on the Atlantic Coast or in the Midwest, while their children are living on the West Coast. On the Pacific Coast, it is estimated that very few children have any available grandparents. The distances within California itself, between north and south, are sufficiently large that when the parents live in Los Angeles and the adult child in northern California the separation is one of 1,000 miles geographically. However, distance is not a significant deterrent for older parents and adult children meetings. Parents or other relatives visit their adult children on vacations, especially around the holidays, and are available on such occasions. When they do not come in a normal course of visiting, however, it is my procedure to have the patient call and invite the parent to come out for the specific purpose of the joint counseling. These parents, therefore, mostly come from considerable distances and since they are going to be here specifically for the purpose of meeting with their adult child, it is well to arrange that they remain several days to a week.

It is always difficult to forecast how much time will be needed to meet together. Generally, it is better to plan on consecutive sessions of several days. While I have met for up to four hours with families in a continuous session, this usually does not work too well because people begin to get tired after two hours of meeting. Another possible arrangement is to have a meeting for two hours in the morning and a meeting for two hours in the afternoon, followed by meetings the following day. It seems more practical from an economic point of view to have the interviews thus crowded together, because usually the relatives do not plan to remain a very long time in the area. Most of them have affairs of their own that they have to attend to.

Most of the time relatives pay their own transportation to the home of the adult child. In cases of financial hardship, however, the child has arranged to pay for the flight ticket of the parent. This is entirely up to the two of them and has never really presented any problem. On one occasion, a parent flew to his adult child's home from a foreign country, but in this case there was sufficient financial ability so that it did not work a hardship.

Strategies

There are certain strategies that one should keep in mind in managing one of these joint sessions. It is important to emphasize to all the family members present that this is a working meeting for everyone. Parents often have the notion that they are to listen to what is happening with their child, and since so many of these families have never really discussed what is going on between them, they tend to sit back and consider it an informational meeting. It is important for the therapist to say immediately that everyone is expected to pitch in, to be thinking about the interactions, and to make new moves to straighten out the problem.

It is also important to clarify constantly what the difficulties are. People may become very wrought up in the discussion and they may remember certain parts of it, but unless the therapist emphasizes what is going on, this may not be clearly understood. For example, where there are misunderstandings that are clarified, it is well to reiterate that this was a misunderstanding, and that the family members can now look at the material in a new light.

It is necessary to continuously ask the patient to state his position but to do so without condemnation of the other family member. If the session begins to tend in the direction of blame, it is well for the therapist to emphasize that the patient is stating his position and that his ideas and his perceptions are his own, that they may not necessarily cover all facts and facets of the situation. If this is not done, there can easily be an accusation–counteraccusation character to the meeting.

The therapist should highlight the problems and clarify any statements by any of the family members that seem significant or, particularly, that point to new information that should be brought up.

One of the goals of a joint session that should be kept in mind is not only a new understanding but a joint, consciously agreed-upon way of handling situations or of relating in the future.

The therapist must often model as a parent for the adult child and his parent. In view of the fact that so many of these families have restricted emotional expression and have not been able to give to one another in a feeling, expressive way, it is well for the therapist to show sympathy, pleasure, concern, or any such emotional response to what comes up in the relationship transactions. This includes helping a family member who is weeping, or being supportive if they become frightened.

It is extremely important to express appreciation to older parents or to siblings who have joined one of these family sessions. In most cases it has taken a good deal of strength for them to go to a meeting, the purpose of which they really do not understand very well, and many of the older parents have no familiarity at all with psychiatric interviews. They may approach them with puzzlement or with apprehension. It is my experience that parents try very hard to be helpful and open through the interviews, and it is well to be clearly appreciative to them. Usually, the adult child is sufficiently embroiled in the emotion of give-and-take of the interview, as well as in much of the material that he has just heard, that he may not make clear his appreciation of the parents' efforts. It frequently happens that at the end of a joint interview, when the therapist thanks the parents for their participation, the parents will turn with considerable emotion and say how much they have appreciated an opportunity to be open about relationships. They often say that they feel the greatest benefit of the meeting has been to themselves.

There is generally a high peak of enthusiasm at the end of one of these joint sessions, and it is well to use the sense of accomplishment and go on to outlining the work for additional meetings, stating clearly what work is to be done in them. The momentum that is gained in joint sessions usually will last through a number of the individual sessions following such a meeting. One can use very profitably the emotion and enthusiasm that is engendered for further meetings with siblings or other family members.

Taping the sessions is useful for both parties as many exchanges are more clearly understood when reheard. Siblings and spouses often gain a new view from listening to tapes also.

Although I have ended the session, I find that parents and child or child and siblings do not end their session. They often will go out to the parking lot and stand talking together for long periods of time. I have observed them from my office window deep in talk for more than two hours. Others have told me that they went for a four-hour lunch, or that they went home and talked until midnight. It is clear that once we have opened the flood gates, the thoughts and feelings stored within them for many years rush out pell-mell and demand expression. The experience is exhilarating but exhausting.

Follow-Up Contacts with Parents

The large majority of parents I see are from other states and live hundreds to thousands of miles away. Consequently, our in-person contacts are limited to a day or to three or four days. Those who live within California are more apt to be in touch with me by telephone and letter. Occasionally, some of these parents have returned for help with their own marital problems. More often their contact with me is motivated by a desire for more suggestions as to how they can be of help to their adult child. For parents, I sometimes assume the role of grandparent, counseling how to manage child–parent relationships.

I receive notes from parents, especially at Christmas time, telling me how they are faring personally, as well as reporting on their relationship with their child. Since parents know I am in contact with their child, their notes tend to be more about their own activities. There are sometimes questions about how to handle some problem that we had discussed in joint sessions. These notes have a feeling of continuity and personal relationship with me and with the process of the meetings. My return notes to them are based on what I think is their accessibility, need for recognition, personal isolation, special uniqueness of their personality, etc. I always express in full my appreciation of their efforts and their help to their child. I also add some brief notes about specific problems that we had jointly discussed and report what progress my patient is making in regard to those problems.

I also receive messages of salutation and progress from the parents through their adult child. The adult child also brings me letters from parents to demonstrate the parents' understanding and changing behavior. I also frequently send my congratulations to the parents via message through the adult child, but this is not as reliable or as effective as writing them myself.

The door is always specifically left open for further get-togethers if any problems arise. Such get-togethers seldom happen as most people have now very clearly in mind what the problems are, and they will normally proceed to work on these relationship frictions themselves. It is a spur to such efforts to know that the possibility of another meeting exists. For example, a patient will say, "I think I and my dad should have another session to discuss. . . . He's doing well but needs some help here and there and I am annoyed about. . . ." I say, "By all means!" The next thing I hear is that the problem has been resolved.

There is an important therapeutic asset that comes to the therapist from these parent–child contacts. While all problems are not resolved, probably, at this point, one knows from an intimate point of view where the parent's difficulty lies. Consequently, one can make pointed suggestions to the patient as to what he can do or say to clarify and to rectify the relationship problem. Neither would be "shooting in the dark."

Follow-Up with the Patient

Immediately after the sessions the patient and I meet as soon as possible to discuss the experience. The patient tells me what his feelings, his observations, and his reactions have been to the whole thing. Usually there is a very lengthy exchange of views between us. It is interesting that we see the transactions essentially alike, although there are certain passages between child and parent that the patient may have missed. I am able to point these out to the patient for his further consideration. The atmosphere of these postsessions is one of pleased excitement, relief, and renewed energy. The patient is now freed of many of his handicapping fears and misunderstandings. His tone is now more tolerant, more forgiving, and sometimes very sad for the position and the personality problems of the parent. The patient has new perspectives, assesses the abilities of the parent more realistically, and reforms his view of what he and the parents can establish between them.

I quote further from John's letter to illustrate such a situation.

> I began to look forward to the sessions. My father's responses surprised me. (1) He did care. (2) He was not aware of the fact that my brother and I called him the Martian Monster because we meant it, "I thought it was a nickname, a joke," and (3) he wanted to know what he could do at this time. It would be a delight to be able to say that my father and I are now able to talk freely with each other and that we have a mutual understanding. Unfortunately, such is not the case. We do have an improved relationship. I understand his rigidity and severe blocking and am sorry he can't enjoy himself more. We talk now about abstractions (it used to be only about things). We talk about philosophy and religion. I enjoy these conversations. I suspect he would like to communicate with me. Even though he can't really, it's nice to know he would like to communicate. Until the sessions, I thought he didn't care.

The most obvious change in the patient's feelings is an absence of the emotional strain and the driving pressure concerning the parental frictions. It has been replaced by a more balanced, realistic awareness of the two sides of the problem relationship. The patient now respects his parents for their efforts to help him in the joint sessions and offers sympathy to the parents for the trials and tribulations that they experienced during the period of his birth and maturation. It may not come to the point of "to understand everything is to forgive everything." Some resentments remain because the hurts were deep, especially if forty years of pain and loneliness, fear and anxiety resulted from family experiences. Many people express a feeling that they have been imprisoned within themselves and have now been released to enjoy the world. But think of the lost years, the lost opportunities!

Here are some more quotes from Carol's letter to illustrate this.

> *It's almost unreal to think back to the person I used to be. I am glad she no longer exists. I guess the greatest thing I gained from our sessions together was a sense of personal worth. It saddens me to think of all those years wasted, feeling inadequate and unloved. But now I know that I* can *do anything if I really try and that people* do *like me and care for me.*
>
> *The strangest part of that interminable hour with my father was that, although I was crying and talking, there was another part inside me observing my father and seeing for the first time what a poor weak person he was. It was the first time I had* really *seen him. From that point on things have gone nowhere but up. I've been able to find the love and praise I need from those around me who really do care and like me and it's wonderful. For this new me, I give thanks.*
>
> Carol

The Rigid Patient

It is not only parents who resist changing. Some patients are quite fixed in their ideas and, in general, rigid in their personality pattern. They are apt to protest that nothing can be altered in their lives because they have had such bad experiences in their childhood family. When such a patient meets with his parent in conjoint interviews to straighten out past and present difficulties, the parent frequently makes changes in attitude and behavior. Some patients resist admitting that there is a change in the parent. They may want to cling to and nourish their hostility toward the parent, or they may wish to retain their rationale for their usual *modus operandi*—it's those experiences when growing up that have permanently "marked" them.

Old ideas and perceptions are often hard to give up. The road to new experiences seems difficult and frightening so it might be better to stay as one is. It is well to recognize and empathize with these feelings of fright and foreboding. Even self-pity cannot be taken away because it is often a major comfort to the person.

While understanding and sympathizing, the therapist can use to advantage the new views gained in the joint sessions to stimulate the patient to continued effort. One can point out that the parent, although many years older, has made changes in outlook and action, which means that his adult child should be able to do so also. Many rigid patients are in a bind with parents over past demands for success that originated in early situations. Patients therefore have a need to fail in order to win out over parents and their old messages requiring achievement. The patients thus preserve their sense of self-determination and individuality, while at the same time maintaining a secret, negative dependency on the parent. The need to fail can be successfully combated by continual reminders that the parent has withdrawn his demands in favor of the patient's self-determinations of his life-style.

Therapists can challenge regressive and denying behavior because a new view of the parent's motivations, feelings, and attitudes has been experienced by both the therapist and the patient. Distortions of the parent's statements or actions can be rectified at once. There may be one or two periods of denial. These denials, or reversions, are apt to occur when the patient has had some kind of setback in his life situation and he finds it tempting to return to old patterns.

Very occasionally, one finds a person with an infantile dependency on the parent, which he does not wish to relinquish. The parent is usually disturbed about such a relationship and will generally be willing to make whatever moves are required to foster independence. Parents, as they grow older, are not eager to take on more responsibilities, for they have graduated from their child-rearing days.

Parents Who Make Little Change

As previously indicated, there are a certain number of parents who are reluctant to come, but very seldom does one absolutely refuse. Of those who do come and join in a joint interview there are about 5 percent, in my experience, who are not capable of any substantive change. Some of them continue to defend their positions, albeit less vociferously. Some of them who verbalized their willingness to change in the joint meetings were really unable to do so, as experience proved. Robert's father, for instance, was seventy-five years old, and a rather feeble man in body, though alert in mind. He had been rigid for many years in his thinking and one would not expect that he would make any marked adjustment. However, there was a modicum of change in him that enabled Robert to get along better with him in the remaining three years of his life. Sylvia's mother, although she was willing to discuss and consider Sylvia's feelings about her attitudes, did not in the long run make many emotional changes. She did make some changes in some very practical things, but as far as her basic attitudes were concerned, time proved that she really was not able to form a close relationship with her daughter.

It is thus possible that family relationships will not be greatly different after the meeting. It is well to have the patient prepared for this in advance of any joint sessions, and to make sure he will be willing to take the chance that his hopes will be dashed, or that a new warm or much closer relationship will result. From thereon, if it has not turned out well, it is a process of mourning for the ideal parent, an ideal he must now relinquish. This process is not substantially different from the mourning that goes on for a parent who has actually died. In such case, there is still an aura of idealism and hope around the deceased parent, although in most families things are not really that perfect. With a parent's death goes the hope of rechanneling and reshaping a parent–child relationship, and along with it there is a real sense of loss and of dismay. The same thing occurs when a parent has tried but cannot change his basic way of operating. There is some difference here in that the patient is much more able to see that it is the parent's inability, rather than his unwillingness, that causes this lack of progress in their relationship.

I quote from two letters that may illustrate this situation more clearly.

> During the interviews in your office, mother wasn't trying to be helpful at all, but it did give me the opportunity to express certain feelings that I wouldn't have otherwise. The results are that when it was over, I understood them better, but I certainly didn't like them any better, not more or less. I realized it wasn't all me that was at fault. It gave me tools to deal with them. I only wish it happened sooner. I did and still do feel pity for my father who is consumed with guilt since her death. When he tries to pass this guilt on to me, I am able to cope and refuse to accept it.
>
> Dagmar

> I was afraid of the loss of my mother's affection. I felt that having kept to myself some of my complaints (for example, my feeling that she favored my brother), the revelation of them to her might provoke hostility. I really didn't know what to do if she should say, "Well, if you feel that way I don't want anything more to do with you." I guess that I really felt deep down she wouldn't cut me off, and so I was willing to go ahead with the session. I must add that my mother, when presented with the idea of the session, was quite compliant, saying she would do anything to help. However, I felt she was scared.
>
> As the session progressed, it appeared to me that my mother was more than willing to be compliant, that she was indulgent of some of my complaints. There were really only two points when I felt she was making contact in terms of sharing feelings, attitudes, etc. The most important was when she had been told several times about the importance of allowing me to express

my own opinions. And she suddenly piped up in a very forceful way, "But I can have my opinions too." The other point was during a discussion of her childhood punishments, etc., and she was defending her protection of my brother. I felt she really meant what she said, believed in what she had done, and felt no shame or guilt in having done so. I felt easier as the session progressed; I thought I was being straightforward and as my mother evinced no hostility I relaxed on that score.

What was accomplished—maybe some honest communication. Maybe some venting of my mother's feelings—not necessarily those directly related to me, but those that festered near her surface for a long time. Maybe some practice for me in being confronting in a supportive situation. After all, I had confidence that had my mother thrown a stinking fit, the therapist was there to smooth things out.

Now weeks after the event I again see evidence that some of the things discussed sank in. For instance, my mother is still not overdoing the telephoning bit. She has refrained from complaining about the grandchildren. I feel more comfortable around my mother and father. I expect my father is still worrying about getting a call from the shrink to invite him to a session. Given his fears of authority figures, and his general hope that my marriage problems were due to something simple like alcohol or women.

Bertha

Even if the parents' attitudes and behavior are not much altered after these joint sessions, a good deal has been gained because the patient has experienced being in a different power relationship. The patient has first of all asked for sharing and consideration on the basis of being a peer, which is quite different from asking for help as a dependent child. He has also found that the parent is now in a different power ranking from what he once was. Now that the child can do without his parent, if he wishes to, the parent is very well aware of this and the transactions within the joint interviews normally make this very clear. An additional change that occurs is that the patient is not only a peer at this point, and an independent personality, but he is joined by a friendly facilitator who will assist him in case there are any unsuccessful binds with the parent. This facilitator also points out things about his parent and brings them to his understanding in a new way. The therapist as a facilitator can do this because he is outside of the regular transactions that go on between the parent and child. Both those individuals are so used to the way that they are relating that it is difficult for them to see outside of their established modes. The therapist, however, adds a different note and in a way acts as the catalyst for a remixing of the older parent and his adult child.

If the family relationships do not improve there is an additional advantage from the experience. The patient has an ideal opportunity to take a look at the roots of his family training, which makes it much clearer to him as to why he is behaving today in the way that he does. This will mean that as he approaches a new relationship, there is a clear concept in his mind of the way he would normally look upon this new encounter, and he may be able to not only intellectually but emotionally make corrections in his approaches to other people in light of his new knowledge and understanding.

Even with those parents who have not made much progress, the adult children usually maintain a surface contact. To the therapist, they verbalize that their relationship with their parent is not the way they would like it, but since the parent cannot change, they wish to maintain some family ties. They do maintain the ties without a great deal of anger and resentment, in contrast to the way they felt before. Their attitude is now apt to be more of regret and sadness than resentment. The case of Sylvia is one that would fall into this category. As that interview indicated, the mother was too defensive to be able to really take a look at her own behavior, or to make a significant move toward Sylvia. Sylvia, however, really wanted to keep in contact with the family and particularly with her father, who was a more benign figure to her. She would not be able to do this unless she made some adjustment in her attitudes toward the mother. They reestablished contact in spite of the stormy joint session.

12

Conclusion

This therapeutic approach is founded on the belief that personality difficulties based on early family interpersonal and interactional experiences that proved to be hurtful or unsuccessful may be improved markedly by utilizing the interactions with the very same persons, in the present time, and in a different context. It is essentially a return to the source of the malfunction and an offering of a milieu for family members to reunite in a healthier way. In typical family therapy, the family member who is exhibiting personal difficulties is either a dependent child or a hospitalized or dependent adult. This discussion concerns independent adults who have been self-sustaining, leading their own lives, and usually having families of their own. These persons may have difficulties in their marriages or in their relationships with others, but they are not to be considered sick in the general meaning. *Sick* implies not functioning at all or just barely functioning, and this is not the category of persons who have been described here. They are called patients in the case examples because psychiatry follows the terminology of the medical model; no agreed-upon terminology yet exists to more appropriately describe such a group.

As the therapist has goals of better functioning for his

patient in a far more satisfactory life for him, so has the family. The family goals for those growing up in its matrix are similarly for a well-functioning, independent adult child. Parents hope that their children will be able to get much out of life—ideally, more than they, the parents, did. The fact that some of these family goals were not met, or that the parents' training of their child went awry, is not reason to eliminate the family as a force.

Nor should it be put in a historical perspective as a fossilized schema of interrelationships. On the contrary, it had vitality and meaning in the past, and it retains that vitality and force if it can be redirected in a more constructive pattern.

The additional positive factor in such a restructuring is the fact that the adult child now has more resources, internal and external, than he had at the outset of life. He has expanded his experiences so that he now has more perspective about himself and other people in the world. As he expanded those experiences, he gained in knowledge of alternative action and thinking. These he employed in dealing with people in situations so that he now is equipped to face a reshaping of family relationships with more tolerance, and yet more capacity for self-assertion.

There is a key factor inherent in older parents and adult children meeting to improve their feelings about one another and to find those new arrangements that mutually satisfy. That key factor is the need of the older parent to maintain a vital link to his adult child, or adult children, for a number of reasons: to maintain a sense of belonging, to have a sense of participating in ongoing life through their grandchildren, to guard against loneliness, to feel that the difficult and uncharted task of parenting was fairly successful, to have a sense of warmth and exchange with their adult child.

Thus the older parent really has more need to strive for a good relationship with his adult child than does his child. The adult child is busy with his own family and is usually very involved in his work and chosen activities. If need be, he could do without his parent. This is quite a different situation from that which obtains for the young child. He cannot do without his parents, or some parental figure. Thus, typical family therapy, which deals with a dysfunctional family and a child exhibiting problems, differs in its alignment of force and power. The adult child often does not emotionally understand that he is now in a strategic position and consequently, on his own he would not utilize the power structure for his benefit. It is the therapist's function in older parent–adult child sessions to closely watch that power structure and try to see to it that both parties gain from the transaction. Having power need not mean that it be used against someone.

Considering the basis of this technique from the psychoanalytic viewpoint, the adult child comes to grips directly with the superego, in the person of the parents who originally set the limits of thought and action. The historical facts of those limitations are perceived by both; the motives for such child training are, largely, only in the awareness of the parent. The child may have speculated and reasoned, but almost never has that child in his adulthood inquired into the intentions and forces behind the parent's message. In these adult child–parent meetings, the child has a developed ego with uneven or distorted perceptions of himself and others. No matter what his trepidations may be about encountering the wrath of parental authority, he has sufficient ego strength to speak as a peer to that authority. The therapist continues to act as a benign authority figure, a counterweight to possible destructive authority.

In this conjoint meeting environment, the self is perceived in a perspective going beyond childhood experiences to the parents' own development and experiences. Information is added that makes past actions and occurrences capable of different assessment. When the adult child states his position on certain problems with the parent, or requests that new arrangements be made with the family, that action is almost always accepted by the parent. There may not be wholehearted agreements, but a working arrangement eventuates. This results in a definite growth in the boundaries of the patient's ego, and a more confident self-perception of "me" and "them." A punitive superego gives way to a more tolerant one.

In family therapy theory, the family arrives at homeostasis in the process of trying to adjust to the various needs, abilities and disabilities, and apprehensions of those in the family group. The struggle to achieve that balance results in family rules that become rigidified by the passage of time. Adult child–older parent confrontations challenge the existing homeostasis; they assert that new forces are present that will not be denied by the old rules, and that new accommodations must be made. Procedurally, the rules are first attacked. Since those rules frequently are not now as applicable as they formerly were during the parent's child-rearing days, there is usually not great resistance to a change. As previously pointed out, the alignment of power is now very different. Even if a parent wishes to stick by the old rules, he soon perceives that it will not work out to his advantage. The parent may well have had changes in his own life experiences—of personal growth, wider understanding of others, more satisfaction in his life—which lessen his demands on others, including his own child. Parents as well as their children continue to grow and develop.

From this point of challenge to the old rules, there are first explanations and historical data, then new perceptions, followed by emotional shifts. New rules are set up by conscious agreement of both sides. A new homeostatic balance begins, which will be tested over a period of time with varying degrees of satisfaction.

Patients strive toward a goal of increased self-esteem, correct perceptions of self and others, capability of entering into mutually enriching emotional relationships, and ability to cope with the events of life. A sense of self-worth is essential to all these goals. Self-worth is socially related and does not exist within a vacuum. A feeling of belonging to a larger whole is an essential ingredient and this may be contributed to by culture, ethnic identity, achievements, and family identity. The need to belong and to identify oneself with a larger whole is evident throughout all our activities. Some types of belonging change during the life cycle, from the teenage cliques to club membership, union affiliation, etc., but the need for identity with family continues. All kinds of human activity attest to this: genealogy investigations, rituals, identification with clans or groups via clothing, heraldry, etc.

In the process of psychotherapy, self-definition and ego growth frequently lead the patient into conflict with parental views, standards, and actions. The individual often feels forced to sever himself from the parents psychologically, if not physically. In the process of separation, the individual feels his parents to be unloving, unkind, lacking in understanding and tolerance. This amounts to feeling that the parent is "bad." The problem is that if one must reject those persons from whom one originated, there is damage to both individual and group self-image.

An additional disadvantage lies in an interrupted sense of continuity. Consider how important the sense of continuity is to us. The child who is named Richard IV has added importance by virtue of those connected with him. If his family has resided in a certain town for three generations, the fact is duly noted as an embellishment to the family and the child. Many a child has been conceived "to carry on the name." Similarly, many of our rituals and habits are continued because they give us a sense of connection with the past.

Including parents in the process of the individual's psychotherapeutic growth is an effective way of promoting self-esteem because it retains the parents as worthwhile persons in the patient's life. His self-esteem is gained not by the sacrifice of theirs but rather by a new accommodation to their joint needs. The conjoint meetings are designed to promote individual self-definition and respect on the part of both parent and child, plus a conscious agreement of how that interchange between them shall be managed for mutual benefit. Such a jointly implemented relationship ensures the sense of worth and continuity of the family. The patient can feel that where he has been was fairly good, where he is now is worthwhile, and he can look forward with more confidence to whatever he may become in the future.

This technique makes great demands upon the therapist's abilities. If one were to look at the requirements of a therapist's abilities in a continuum or a spectrum, the therapist–patient dyad is the least demanding. There is only one person besides himself to watch and think about. Most therapists do quite well in such circumstances. Group therapy adds a number of extra persons to think about, plus the group process itself. Some may contend that conjoint marital therapy is less taxing than group therapy, but there is an essential difference. The marital couple has a very important contract between them, and everything that happens adds to or detracts from that emotional contract. One may become angry at group members, or leave the group in disgust, without the same sense of loss as one has in a marriage situation. Family therapy, which includes dependent children, is yet more complex and requires even more flexibility, alertness to verbal and nonverbal behavior, trend of group feeling, etc.

Having had much experience with all these modes of therapy, I find that joint family sessions with older parents and adult children are the most taxing of all. Emotions seem to rise higher—or fall lower—and intensity of reactions seems far more heightened than in any other situation. For this reason, it seems advisable that only well-trained and experienced persons undertake such interviews. Considerable experience in family therapy with dependent children should certainly be a prerequisite. In addition, the therapist should be willing to place himself in situations that are intensely emotional and in which he may have to take swift and decisive action. Reference is here made to the case example in which the mother and daughter had to be separated or possibly physical combat would have been the conclusion of the encounter.

No one is too old to change. Age has nothing to do with ability to see new vistas or try new roads, as long as the desire and the willingness to venture forth exists. Older parents, in my experience, are willing to take a chance for change. Their abilities to follow through are variable, of course, but most do make some alterations. For those who try and cannot achieve a real change in their relationship to their adult child, all is not lost. The adult child is able to see that he will have to reorganize his thinking and feeling about his parent, and if separation of feeling and contact is necessary, it is done in a spirit of mourning and regret. The perspective gained in the parent–child joint sessions is helpful in that it no longer is necessary or useful to go through old resentments or reiterate hurts. There is a substantial difference in perceiving that the parent who doesn't change is behaving so not out of willfulness or hostility but rather because of incapacity. Most persons who feel their childhood families hurt them feel that it was conscious or deliberate on the part of parents and aimed at them. Usually, it was due to other factors overwhelming the parent, or to some incapacities of his own.

While such reassessment is of great value, there are other positive gains available to the adult patient via this method. It is useful experience in constructive confrontation, something that a great many persons do poorly, mostly because they do not know how to go about it. Many families have continuous confrontations, but nothing comes out of them but hurt feelings and resentment or hopelessness. These confrontations tend to be repetitious, and without an objective outsider they do not take new directions. The experience gained in such a constructive parent–child confrontation is apt to spill over beneficially into other life situations that should be met directly. Nothing succeeds like success, and those who have had a successful encounter with the parent feel strengthened and more self-confident that they can duplicate the success elsewhere. In general, this is true, and many veterans of such meetings have gone about the straightening out of other personal entanglements with positive results.

It is also good experience in dealing with reality. Much of what goes on in families gets to be myth or ritual. Dependent children are not in a position to do much challenging of such rituals or to debunk family myths. Adult children, however, are much better situated to do just that. If parents try to maintain the old system, the therapist is the assistant who points out the realities of the exchange. This is the point at which the therapist should be on the alert, however, because the adult child may slide along in the old, established grooves of family behavior if it seems too difficult to stop the procedure. Reality of feeling, reality of experience is the basis on which parent and child will need to reorient themselves. Most joint sessions lay the groundwork and set the tone for this kind of basic work. Again, this experience widens out into other personal contacts with beneficial results.

This method of psychotherapy does not always result in smoothly functioning family relationships, but it is a very useful tool, which may bring the above benefits. It also tends to speed up the patient's progress. It seems evident that as long as the therapist hears only the adult patient's version of his childhood training, he may be listening to a skewed report. Not that the adult patient is consciously distorting. What he may not realize is that there were other crucial factors operating in the situation that he did not know about for various reasons. He may have seen only the tip of the iceberg, or maybe a corner of it. Consequently, many perceptions of the patient about his parents' behavior toward him may be correct, but the reasons that he gives for that behavior may be incorrect. As some previous case examples illustrated, misunderstandings are common in families, and a whole superstructure of belief may be built up on only part of the parents' course of action or attitude. It may even be the least representative part of that action. These family misunderstandings tend to get more and more involved, and from some simple first event, a whole mass of misunderstandings evolves. Including older parents is, therefore, beneficial in making the whole episode, which parents and child experienced, clearer and more available for useful change.

These experiences have particular value for those marital situations where spouses are unconsciously carrying on the unsuccessful relationship patterns learned from their parents. The objectionable behavior in the marriage can now be seen as an outcome of early training and not as an innately hostile or uncaring attitude. In such cases, relearning may take place, with the older parent's participation, much more quickly and directly than through traditional individual or joint marital counseling. "You're just like your father (mother)" can now become not an epithet or a condemnation but a reason for therapeutic work for reevaluation and for reshaping of feelings and attitudes.

A positive aspect of this method is the benefit it brings to older parents. They have an opportunity to clarify with their child that they want to be of help, and to prove that they want to benefit him as much as possible. Where there has been friction, there is a chance to eliminate it and be on a better footing. The growth of warmth and understanding between older parents and their children is very precious to them. They often express their appreciation for being asked to come to a joint session because they are eager for good relationships with their child. It is also one way for them to be able to give to their adult child, who otherwise is now quite self-sufficient. And lastly, it is a validation that they themselves are a vital force, still important to their child, and that with joint efforts they maintain significant relationships and vital participation in the family.

I quote from two letters that express participants' attitudes about such meetings—from an adult child and from a parent. Both describe essential elements of the procedure. I include almost the entire letter from Babette because it includes so much of the whole procedure—the apprehension, the process, the identity problems, the changing relationship, and the final outcome.

> Last year[1] when my dad and I came in to see you I was in pretty bad shape. I had asked him not to come and visit. I didn't want to see him. But as usual he ignored my wishes and came anyway. I think I started to argue with him the moment he arrived. When we got to your office I was very angry and very much on the defensive.
>
> For many years I had wanted to throw all kinds of shit at him to let him know what he had done to me (It was all his fault, right!) But I could never really do it. Fear of some kind held me back. I guess it was the fear that I might learn that he really didn't love me. I could never handle that. Well, in your office I was allowed to vent my feelings, I wasn't afraid any more. The strange thing about it was, here I am, a 36 year old woman screaming at her dad like a six or seven year old. But I really felt like a little girl, as though I was 30 years younger, like a small child trying to get through to her daddy. I was actually reliving a portion of my past, as if I were really there. Well it worked, the six year old got rid of a lot of shit and the 36 year old functions a hell of a lot better. He's still not the father I would have liked, but I can now accept the fact that he is a man with limitations and hang ups of his own, and they are his, not mine. He never will be able to hug me or give me the things that I needed. Even if he could, they would no longer count. It's the six year old in me that needed that, not the adult.
>
> So I guess what I learned is two things. Acceptance of my dad, and the realization that he did what he could with what he had and in his way he loves me. The other is acceptance of myself. The past is gone, over, done with. I can't bring it back. Today and tomorrow are new days. Some are going to be rough–but I'll get through. They can never get as bad as they used to, they can only get better. There are smiles and good feelings out there, and I'm beginning to demand some. They have my name on them. They belong to me.
>
> What it did for my dad is amazing. You penetrated that hard shell. I've only

[1]This letter was from several years ago.

seen it broken once before. When you brought tears to his eyes[2] you opened some kind of door that has been shut for many many years, and it's still open. He and I communicate better. So does he and his son. He even visits his sisters, they weren't on speaking terms for a long time. In other words, I can see some warmth in him, he's a little more human.

That's where we are now. There is no where else to go but UP.

Babette

This mother describes her meeting with her son. She had spent nearly sixty years feeling that she must be helpful to others, even though that required taking responsibilities she would rather not have had. Needing to please others often meant she had to put her own feelings second. Her efficient assumption of responsibility set a high standard for her son, who began to feel more and more insecure about his ability to measure up and to please her. The sessions gave them both quite a different view of each other's feelings.

I recall that my first reaction, when Larry told me of your request for my presence at one of his sessions with you, was one of astonishment. Larry had been having emotional problems for years now—off and on. Many times I have gone over in my mind the probable causes and the role I have played in his life. I didn't feel that I had exerted undue influence, for he had been quite independent, so I thought, in most of his decisions in life, and had achieved as well, a certain early financial independence, i.e., paper routes, part time jobs and scholarships. I had worked hard for both my sons and my devotion appeared unquestionable. Still I went back over the much trod ground mentally again, albeit rather wearily. Nothing new emerged.

I flew to my son's home on a Sunday and we had a family reunion with both sons and their wives. Our interview was set up for Tuesday; one hour with me first, and then two hours with Larry and me. My daughter-in-law had expressed her apprehension for me over the coming interview, and strangely enough that completely restored my confidence; and now my son's need was paramount!

The next two hours were more gruelling, for Larry and I came to grips with reality and we revealed things to each other that we probably never would have. A veil was stripped from our eyes and we saw what we had never seen before. Much to my utter horror, I realized that Larry had spent much of his

[2] When I mentioned his deceased wife, Babette's mother.

life trying to please me! Dear God, that was the very last thing in this world that I want! Unconsciously I had programmed him just as others had programmed me! Ugh! And we both had been striving to please everybody except ourselves.

At the close of the interview, Dr. Lee did (to my mind) an amazing thing. She came over to my chair, and put her arms around me, much as one would comfort a weeping child.[3] She asked Larry to do the same. I was exhausted and quite ready to call a halt.

During the rest of the week that I was at my son's home, and as a direct result of that session Larry and my daughter-in-law and I had many a talk session. We all were able to express ourselves more honestly and we were able to shed our roles as parent or child and speak from the heart, as adult individuals. The inhibitions that our respective roles in life had imposed on us were unimportant and honesty and the truth were paramount. Consequently, we became very close and Larry and I discovered, I think, that we not only loved each other very much, but that we also liked each other even more!

Mrs. Norma R.

---

[3] She was indeed weeping heavily.

Index

Ackerman, Nathan, 22, 34
Adler, Alfred, 19-20
adversary situation, 48
anger, 80, 81, 86, 87, 125, 127, 137, 177
anxiety, 109, 116, 136, 171
authority (parental-like) figure, 18

Bateson, Gregory, 22
behavior modification, 27

children's rights, 32-33
communication, 23, 32, 35, 36, 39, 40, 47, 61, 71, 96, 106, 131, 135, 141, 142, 149, 155, 158, 176
conflict, 130-134
confrontation, 49, 93, 96, 105, 112, 113, 117, 122, 128, 142, 143, 157-158, 165, 176, 182, 185-186
conjoint family therapy, 22, 23, 71, 146, 157-161

conjoint meeting, 61, 135, 157-160, 181
parent-child, 43-61, 68-72, 74-77, 87, 145, 184
counseling, 51

depression, 56, 59, 73, 79, 80-87, 91, 109, 116, 126, 131, 142, 149, 151
Depression (Great, 1930s), 32, 33, 107
discipline, 63, 67, 113-116, 156
"double-bind," 22-23
drives
   emotional, 18
   instinctual, 18

ego, 18, 181-182, 183
   development of, 24
encounter, 57, 128, 149, 185
extramarital affairs, 72-78, 97-101

family
  childhood, 18, 34, 37, 38, 44, 64, 65-66, 87, 97, 150, 153, 155, 172, 185
  goals, 31-33, 35, 180
  history, 45, 105, 133, 140, 142
  rules, 96, 103, 133, 182
  systems, 24, 27, 31, 38, 43, 103
  therapy, *see* therapy, family
  training, 177
fight training, 65
free association, 18
Freud, Sigmund, 18-19
friction
  family, 156-161
  parental, 171
frigidity, 66

group
  encounter, 20-22
  encounter addict, 21-22
  couples, 26
growth, emotional, 18-19
Gurman, Alan, 25

Haley, Jay, 22
hippie culture, 32
homeostasis, 24, 182
homosexual(ity), 140, 145-146

impotency, 66
incest, 140-145
individuality, 35, 36
individual problems, 79
insight, 34, 44
interaction, 20, 23, 167, 179
  emotional, 37, 129, 150
  parent-child, 21, 86
  sibling-child, 21
interrelationships, 180

Jackson, Don, 22
joint counseling, 46, 47, 130, 135, 186

joint counseling (*cont.*)
  family, 92, 95-96, 132-133, 163-177, 184
  marital, 139-153
  parent-child, 56-61, 68-72, 74-77, 81, 86, 87, 88-93, 98-101, 103-123, 126-128, 130-133, 137-140, 146, 166, 181, 185
  sibling, 95-102, 150, 152-153, 154-155
Judeo-Christian ideas, 33

life situations, 20
life-style, 32, 34, 64, 165, 173
"Lockheed syndrome," 148

marital counseling, 26, 63, 147, 187
  problems, 56, 64, 72, 79, 112, 113, 132, 133, 153-155, 169
  therapy, 25, 63-78, 106, 120
marriage system, 29
  basis of, 33
  crises, 31
martyr, 119-123

open marriage, 66
operant conditioning, 27
oversensitivity, 86

Parents Without Partners, 149
Peoplemaking, 23
personality, 41, 79, 92, 155, 170, 176
projections, 18
psychiatry, 17, 164, 179
psychoanalysis, 18-19, 22
psychological counseling, 37
psychotherapeutic change, 34
psychotherapy, 17-20, 23, 26, 36, 86-87, 183, 186
  goals of, 34-39
  group, 20-22

Index 193

relationships, 20, 25, 34, 35, 36-37, 41, 44-45, 47, 48, 50, 52, 54, 61, 64, 65, 79, 95, 128, 142, 146, 151, 179, 182
   family, 92-93, 111-112, 140, 144-145, 156-157, 174, 177, 180, 186
   male-female, 66-67, 72, 78, 98, 99, 100, 125, 137, 139
   marital, 136-139
   parent-child, 50, 77, 85, 86, 88, 116, 137, 139, 142, 145, 168, 169, 170, 174, 175, 188
   sibling, 150, 154-155
religion, 132
religious counselors, 25
rituals, 183

sadomasochistic practices, 146
Satir, Virginia, 7-9 (Foreword), 23
schizophrenic, 22
self, 92-93, 181, 182
self-awareness, 35
self-esteem, 31, 35, 80, 140, 141, 142, 145, 182, 183-184
semiparental role, 51
sexual attitudes, 136
sexual problems, 66, 97-102, 135-146

sharing, 31, 35, 36, 64, 67
social identity, 147
stress, 31, 35, 36
Sullivan, Harry S., 20
superego, 24, 25, 181-182
surrogate parental role, 35

taping sessions, 168-169
therapy, 35, 41, 55, 56, 80, 88, 113
   couple, 157
   couple group, 26-27
   family, 24, 44, 80, 93, 179, 181, 182, 184
   group, 27, 144, 146, 149, 184
   individual, 26, 44, 97, 119, 146, 157
transactions, 20, 24, 26-27, 36, 80, 103-123, 168, 176
   emotional, 21
   parent-child, 71, 172, 177, 181
transference, 18, 48
Treating the Troubled Family, 34 (fn)
trust, 48-49

Weakland, John, 22
"workaholic," 63
World War II, 32